Parivartana Yogas are said to be among the most powerful of planetary combinations, having the capacity to link the effects of two astrological houses in a chart. However, aside from what we find explicitly in Mantreswara's *Phala Deepika*, there's little in the literature – neither in the many classics of *Jyotisha*, nor in modern books – to help us understand these yogas. So we begin with definitions.

Definitions

The word *yoga* itself means "yoke, or union". In *Jyotisha*, a yoga is formed, with only a few single-planet exceptions, when two or more planets are joined in a specific configuration or relationship.

The word *parivartana* has many meanings. To include just a pertinent few from the Monier-Williams' *Sanskrit-English Dictionary*, for example, we have:
- turning or whirling around
- rolling about, moving to and fro
- inverting, putting in a reverse order
- barter, exchange, return

In essence, *parivartana* connotes mobility and movement, but only in the sense that the planets are symbolically mobile. A *Parivartana Yoga* has nothing to do with travel *per se*, but by implication, a *Parivartana Yoga* is dynamic, because the two planets are linked in a manner that allows transposition by sign and, therefore, by house.

A *Parivartana Yoga* occurs when one planet occupies a sign whose lord is in the sign ruled by the other planet. In other words, Planet A occupies a sign ruled by Planet B, while

Planet B occupies a sign ruled by Planet A.

For example, consider the Moon in Aquarius while Saturn is in Cancer. The Moon resides in one of Saturn's signs while Saturn resides in the Moon's sign. This creates a bond, or *sambandha* between the Moon and Saturn. More specifically, for an Aries ascendant it would create a *Parivartana Yoga* linking the 4th and 11th houses, since these are the houses directly occupied and exchanged.

Note: Although Saturn also rules the 10th house of Capricorn, the Moon does not occupy the 10th, so our range of interpretation would be restricted to an intertwining of the 4th and 11th houses.

This phenomenon of reciprocal sign occupation often goes under the name of "exchange". The two planets effectively swap signs, just as two owners of time-share condos might, as arranged through their co-op administration, live in each other's condo to experience the benefits of a different locale. Thus, both parties enjoy a "non-localized" experience otherwise unavailable to them.

In Western astrology, this is commonly referred to as "mutual reception". Again, the words themselves add nuance. One planet is receptive to another who reciprocates in kind. For example, Canada maintains an embassy in the USA which, in turn, maintains an embassy in Canada. Diplomacy is thus facilitated, presumably to the benefit of both countries, because they're mutually receptive to each other's concerns.

The exchange of house lords invokes the cooperation of their respective houses. But as we all know, the nature of houses varies significantly. Broadly speaking, we can thus divide houses into two distinct groups:

- Positive houses include the *kendras* or angular houses (1-4-7-10), the *trikonas* or trinal houses (5-9) and the so-called neutral houses (2-11).

- Negative houses include the *dusthanas* (3-6-8-12).

Of the latter group, we can further distinguish between what are called "serious" *dusthanas*, ie, the *trikasthanas* (6-8-12), and the "mild" *dusthana* of the 3rd house. The *trik* houses are problematic under most circumstances, and are considered undesirable locations for any planet. Somewhat better is the 3rd house, which is an *upachaya bhava* (house) representing difficulties at the outset, but also promising improvement over time proportionate to effort.

The various exchanges of house lords can thus be grouped into three distinct categories of yoga, each with a more specific designation:

Maha Parivartana Yoga

Maha means "dignified, exalted, glorious, majestic, nobly born." A *Maha Parivartana Yoga* therefore implies a touch of divine fortune.

The yoga involves the mutual exchange of any two positive house lords, ie, the lords of houses 1-2-4-5-7-9-10-11. There are 28 such possible combinations. Generally speaking, these yogas confer positive results for both participant houses, the degree of which is subject to other considerations to be discussed later. Mantreswara said of this yoga:

> *The native born with a Maha Yoga in his birth chart will be endowed with the blessings of the Goddess Shri, will have enormous wealth, will have garments of variegated colors, wear gold ornaments, will be richly rewarded by the sovereign with gifts and administrative authority, and possess vehicles, wealth and children.* (Phala Deepika 6:34)

In this quotation, we see another key element of classical exegesis, that of *arthavada*, or eulogy. As is the practice of many classical authors, Mantreswara provides a laudatory description of the multiple benefits accruing to the fortunate possessor of a *Maha Parivartana* Yoga. Should we take him literally and expect that every client with this yoga will enjoy good fortune, wealth, governmental favor and beautiful children?

No, we shouldn't be misled into thinking this is a literal interpretation. Mantreswara merely intends to impress upon us that this is a *good* yoga and that, given the appropriate support, it will generate benefits of some kind or other in the life of the individual.

Khala Parivartana Yoga

Khala means "abusive, contentious, mischievous, quarrelsome, villainous, wicked." A *Khala Parivartana Yoga* therefore implies something of a troublemaker.

The yoga involves the mutual exchange of the 3rd house lord with any one of the positive house lords, ie, houses 1-2-4-5-7-9-10-11. There are eight such possible combinations. Generally speaking, these yogas confer mixed results for the participant houses, subject to time, effort and the condition of the house lords themselves. Here again, Mantreswara comments:

> *The native born with a Khala Yoga in his birth chart is sometimes haughty and at times very gentle and polite. His life is dotted with both success and failures. At times he has God's plenty and at another he is in distress, poverty, misery and the like.* (Phala Deepika 6:33)

Dainya Parivartana Yoga

Dainya means "affliction, depression, misery, wretchedness." A *Dainya Parivartana Yoga* therefore implies difficulties and misfortunes.

The yoga involves the mutual exchange of any *trik* lords, ie, the lords of houses 6-8-12, among themselves and with any lord of the remaining houses, ie, 1-2-3-4-5-7-9-10-11. There are

30 such possible combinations. Generally speaking, these yogas confer negative results for the participant houses, the degree of which is also subject to other considerations. Again, in Mantreswara's words:

> The native born with a Dainya Yoga in his birth chart is a fool, speaks ill of others, always acting sinfully, tormented by his enemies, always hurts the feelings of others by his speech and is of unstable mind. Whatever he ventures, it is full of hurdles. (Phala Deepika 6:33)

Again, in a passage as damning as this, we must remember this is an example of *arthavada*, where eulogy is balanced by condemnation. Will every client with a *Dainya Yoga* be a foul-mouthed neurotic loser tormented by foes and circumstances alike? No, but he will experience difficulties subject, and proportionate, to other fixed karmas indicated in his chart.

The mathematics of *Parivartana Yogas*

As noted above, the 12 house lords of the chart are capable of forming 66 combinations of exchange, which render the full spectrum of *Parivartana Yogas* – 28 *Maha yogas*, eight *Khala yogas*, and 30 *Dainya yogas*.

Although 66 combinations are possible, only 57 are available for any given ascendant. Of the nine excluded, examination of any chart will reveal these following – five by virtue of dual rulership, and four by virtue of astronomical limitation:

- Mars, Mercury, Jupiter, Venus and Saturn each own two houses in a chart but, by definition, can't exchange places with itself. For example, for an Aries ascendant, there's no exchange between the 1st and 8th houses because Mars rules both. Likewise, the 3rd and the 6th are both ruled by Mercury, the 9th and 12th by Jupiter, the 2nd and 7th by Venus, and the 10th and 11th by Saturn. Similar logic applies to every other ascendant. Thus, five yoga combinations are excluded – one for each dual house lord.

- Because the orbits of Mercury and Venus lie within that of the Earth's, their apparent angular separations from the Sun cannot exceed 28 and 48 degrees of longitude, respectively. Therefore, there can be no exchange between the lords of Leo and Gemini (Sun and Mercury), or Leo and Taurus (Sun and Venus). Thus, another two combinations are excluded.

- By the same token, it's impossible for Mercury and Venus to be separated by more than (28 + 48 =) 76 degrees. Therefore, there can be no exchange between the lords of Taurus and Virgo (Venus and Mercury), or Gemini and Libra (Mercury and Venus). Thus, yet another two combinations are excluded.

Exchanges among the five true planets are the most common. Technically, the Sun is a star, and the Moon a satellite, while the true planets – aside from Earth – are Mercury, Venus, Mars, Jupiter and Saturn. They each own two signs and, except for Mercury and Venus, are unrestricted in their freedom of angular separation. Exchanges are least common between (a) the Sun and the Moon because they own only one sign each, and (b) the Sun and Mercury or Venus because of their orbits as described above.

The exchange uncertainty principle

In quantum physics, the Heisenberg Uncertainty Principle presents a paradox. It states that, in the realm of atomic particles, you can't know everything. You can know the particle's exact position but not its exact energy state, or know its energy state but not its position. Not both at the same time.

Thanks to the oscillatory nature of the planetary exchange, the *Parivartana Yoga* is equally dynamic. On paper we see the planets in their true astronomical positions. But in our mind's eye we can also see them in their hypothetical positions – post-exchange – in their own signs.

On a gross level, each planet switches to the other sign with no degree of particularity. In practice, however, there are two different ways of imagining a planet's post-exchange position. At this more subtle level, once we take into account their specific degrees, we'll see that the *Parivartana Yoga* is potentially more complex than previously imagined.

Planets in identical degrees:

The simplest case is when the two planets in exchange occupy the same degree position in their respective signs, eg, Saturn at 13 Aries, Mars at 13 Capricorn. Under exchange, Saturn moves from 13 Aries to 13 Capricorn, while Mars moves from 13 Capricorn to 13 Aries.

Yet one or both of these planets may be in eclipse, combustion or planetary war, each configuration contingent upon degree proximity to another luminary or planet. If one is combust, post-exchange the other will probably be too. If one is in planetary war, post-exchange the other will likely meet the same fate.

Bear in mind these are general statements. The caveats are that (a) only the Moon is eclipsed by the Sun, (b) different planets become combust at varying degrees of proximity to the Sun, and (c) planetary war only applies between true planets.

But you get the general idea. If your house is on fire, and we exchange houses, I'll be on fire too – unless I'm wearing an asbestos suit.

Planets in different degrees:

A far more common dynamic emerges when the two planets occupy different degrees in their respective signs. The greater that difference, the more likely that, aside from sign occupation, the pre-exchange and post-exchange conditions could be dramatically modified.

Let's say in this case, Saturn is at 25 Aries, Mars at 13 Capricorn. When these two exchange positions in our mind's eye, should each swap their degree positions with that of the other, or should they carry their degree positions with them? In other words, should a planet in exchange occupy only the footprint left by its exchange partner, or should it create a new footprint in the other sign?

Which of these two post-exchange positions should apply? Without trying to be evasive, we might say both. Whether you accept this answer or not is a measure of your ability to hold ambiguity in your mind.

Exchanging degree position:

Under both sign and degree exchange, Saturn leaves 25 Aries and assumes Mars' position at 13 degrees Capricorn. Likewise, Mars leaves 13 Capricorn and assumes Saturn's position at 25 Aries.

Let's assume Mars at 13 Capricorn was in planetary war, while Saturn at 25 Aries is combust. If we allow the planets to step into each other's exact degree position, what affected one will likely now affect the other, taking into account the caveats mentioned above.

Transferring degree position:

But if we allow each planet to carry its own degree position into the sign exchanged, it might well escape the fate the other previously suffered. Yet, at the same time, it may step onto a landmine that had lain undisturbed by the other planet in the exchange.

If you think there's no distinction between these two options, let's add a few additional players to this hypothetical chart: Venus at 13 Aries, the Sun at 25 Aries, and Jupiter at 13 Capricorn.

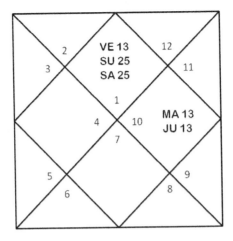

Under the first exchange scenario (swapping degrees), Saturn goes from 25 Aries to 13 Capricorn. It escapes debilitation and combustion but ends up in planetary war. Meanwhile, Mars goes from 13 Capricorn to 25 Aries. It forfeits exaltation, escapes planetary war, but ends up combust.

Under the second scenario (transferring degrees), Saturn goes from 25 Aries to 25 Capricorn. It escapes debilitation in Aries but avoids planetary war in its own sign. Meanwhile, Mars goes from 13 Capricorn to 13 Aries. Although it forfeits exaltation in Capricorn, it eludes combustion in its own sign, but winds up in planetary war with Venus.

One might think this a needless complication, but *Parivartana Yoga* is already an exercise in imagining "what if?" these planets exchange signs. It's not an astronomical reality. It's a hypothetical construct that allows us to see a new pattern based on planetary symbiosis. Like everything else in *Jyotisha*, the consideration of such details may lend useful nuance to our interpretations.

Evaluation of planets using *avasthas*

Given the examples above, we now understand that planets can exist in different states – positive, negative or neutral – before and after their exchange. It's therefore useful to have a means by which we can assess the state of the participant planets and thus the *gestalt* of the exchange itself. Fortunately, the system of *avasthas* provides the discretionary lens through which we can view the planets.

The Sanskrit term *avastha* means "state" or "condition". In the Vedanta tradition, the word *avastha* is used to describe the three most common states of consciousness: waking (*jagrat*), dreaming (*svapna*), and sleep (*sushupti*).

In *Jyotisha*, several *avastha* systems qualify the condition of planets. The well-known *Baladi Avastha* system is based on a planet's longitude within one of five ranges in each sign. In odd signs, these reflect "states" of infancy (0-6 degrees), adolescence (6-12 degrees), youth (12-18 degrees), old age (18-24 degrees), and death (24-30 degrees). In even signs, the order is reversed.

For our purposes, however, we'll use a more general set of *avasthas* based on a planet's occupation by sign, and its astronomical condition irrespective of sign. The list below identifies these dozen *avasthas*:

<u>*Avastha* – Descriptive meaning – Technical meaning</u>

Pradipta – Exulting, blazing – Exaltation sign

Sukhita – Happy – *Moolatrikona* sign

Svastha – Own – Own sign

Mudhita – Delighted – Sign of a friend

Shanta – Peaceful – Sign of a natural benefic

Shakta – Powerful, capable – Retrograde

Khala – Base, low – Sign of a natural malefic

Vikala – Imperfect, marred – Sign of an enemy

Nipidita – Tortured, defeated – Planetary war

Atibhita – Very frightened – Debilitated

Sudhuhkita – Very distressed – Combust

Kopa – Infirm, eclipsed – Eclipsed

For the Moon, which is never subject to planetary war, we can add two other *avasthas*, one positive and one negative:

- (+) Full Moon, ie, "full-ish" being opposite the Sun or within one sign on either side of that opposition

- (-) New Moon, ie, "new-ish" being conjunct the Sun or within one sign on either side of that conjunction

In practice, we can expedite our planetary analysis by restricting the *avasthas* under consideration. By culling this list, I'm not suggesting certain *avasthas* are meaningless, only that some are less vital to the analysis, eg, planets in *moolatrikona* (already covered as own sign), planets in signs of benefics/malefics, and planets in signs of friends/enemies.

By the same token, we could also add to the list. For example, an important qualitative measure is *dig bala* – a planet's directional strength. After exclusions and additions, our core list of *avasthas* (four positive, four negative) now looks like this:

Strong planet	Weak planet	Moon phase
+ Own sign	- Debilitation	+ strong within one sign of full
+ Exaltation	- Combust	
+ Retrograde	- Planetary war	- weak within one sign of new
+ *Dig bala*	- Eclipse	

For those unfamiliar with the definitions of these terms, please refer to Appendix 1.

Aside from this abridged set of *avasthas*, we can also consider a few other variables in the analysis of *Parivartana Yogas*: the exchange of benefics vs malefics, *guna* lords and relative house lords. Although these other considerations are less vital than the *avasthas* themselves, they're still capable of adding nuance to an interpretation.

Natural benefics and malefics

By virtue of their lordship of positive or negative houses, the three types of *Parivartana Yoga* already take into account the functional nature of planets. But we can also glean additional meaning from the benefic or malefic nature of participant planets:

- Venus and Jupiter are unconditional benefics. In other words, their benign nature does not change under any circumstances.

- The Sun, Mars and Saturn are unconditional malefics. Their malignant nature does not change under any circumstances. (Noted earlier: the nodes are also unconditional malefics but are left out of this discussion because they don't form *Parivartana Yogas*.)

- The Moon and Mercury are conditional benefics. Their nature depends upon their circumstances:

  - The Moon is a benefic when more than six *tithis* (72 degrees) away from the Sun; otherwise it's a malefic.

  - Mercury is a benefic if it: (1) stands alone in a sign, (2) is influenced only by natural benefics, or (3) is influenced by natural malefics but also by natural benefics that are stronger. Otherwise it is a malefic.

For *Maha Parivartana Yogas* (fortunate), an exchange of natural benefics may further enhance the positive meanings of these yogas, perhaps through harmonious, enlightened or socially-acceptable circumstances.

An exchange of natural malefics may still render positive results, but the planets' malefic nature might emerge through self-serving, aggressive, traumatic or unethical actions or circumstances.

An exchange between a benefic and malefic may be colored by circumstances according to which planet exerts greater strength, although the outcome will likely be positive, as expected for this category of yoga.

For *Dainya Parivartana Yogas* (unfortunate), an exchange of natural benefics may somehow soften the negative consequences of these yogas, perhaps through well-intended actions turning in poor results.

On the other hand, an exchange of natural malefics may amplify the negative results expected via circumstances that go from bad to worse.

An exchange between a benefic and malefic may be colored according to which planet exerts greater strength, although the outcome will likely be negative, as expected.

The *gunas*

We can also consider the *gunas* of the participating planets. In Sanskrit, *guna* means "strand", "quality" or "constituent." In Yoga and Samkhya traditions, it refers to the triad of forces – *sattva*, *rajas* and *tamas* – thought to be the building blocks of nature. Patanjali, author of the famous *Yoga Sutras*, said the *gunas* have dispositions, respectively, for brightness, activity, and inertia. Other interpreters have used terms such as balance, mobility, and inertia.

The planets can be grouped by *gunas*, in accordance with their natures:

- The Sun, Moon and Jupiter are *sattvik*. They represent principles of self-awareness, mental calm and spiritual devotion.

- Mercury and Venus are *rajasik*. They evoke activity, communication, commerce and relationships.

- Mars and Saturn are *tamasik*. They personify inertia, sloth, materialism and violence. (Note: Rahu and Ketu are also *tamasik*, but don't generate *Parivartana Yogas*.)

With the *gunas* in mind, we can interpret an exchange accordingly. If one *guna* dominates, its nature may prevail. Let's assume Mercury and Venus are in a *Parivartana Yoga*. Since both are active and mobile *rajasik* planets, we might expect the yoga to manifest readily.

Conversely, if *tamasik* Mars and Saturn are in exchange, the yoga may manifest only with difficulty, because the nature of the *guna* is inertia.

Where two different *gunas* are involved, we can examine the planets to assess relative strengths or weaknesses, and thus identify the *guna* likely to dominate the outcome.

We might also describe variations on a theme according to the dominant *guna*. *Sattvik* planets in a *Maha Parivartana Yoga* may suggest good things happening effortlessly as a result of positive karma. *Rajasik* planets in the same yoga may imply positive results as a direct consequence of personal effort. But with *tamasik* planets, we might resign ourselves to long-term gain only after time, trials and traumas have exacted their toll.

Relative house lords

We can also consider the relative house positions of planets in exchange. "Relative position" means we ignore absolute house numbers, but count houses as being X/Y houses removed from each other. For example, take the 1st house and 5th houses. When we count (inclusively) from 1st to 5th, we get five houses removed. When we count (always forward, and inclusively) from 5th to 1st, we get nine houses removed. Thus the 1st and the 5th are said to be in a 5/9 relationship.

Following are some general themes for this limited number of exchange variations:

- Relative lords 1/7, themes of relationship and partnership, negotiation and arbitration, marriage and war.

- Relative lords 2/12, themes of family and foreigners, sustenance and loss, net worth and expense, knowledge and self-undoing.

- Relative lords 3/11, themes of siblings and friends, desire and ambition, effort and income, communication and community.

- Relative lords 4/10, themes of mothers and managers, education and career, home and profession, happiness and social status.

- Relative lords 5/9, themes of children and fathers, gurus and disciples, study and authorship, creativity and spirituality.

- Relative lords 6/8, themes of conflict and trauma, service and transformation, lawsuits and legacies, illness and disease.

Other participating yogas

Under certain circumstances, two planets in exchange will also form some other kind of yoga for that chart. Eg, within the *Maha Parivartana Yogas* (exchange of positive house lords), consider only the following scenarios involving the *lagnesh*, or ascendant lord:

- Exchange of the 1st with the 4th, 5th, 7th, 9th or 10th lords is also a *Dharma Karma Adhipati Yoga*, suggesting power and success arising from a fortunate combination of effort and luck.

- Exchange of the 1st with the 2nd or 11th lords is also a *Dhana Yoga*, suggesting accumulation and wealth.

- From these two examples alone, we can see that certain exchanges of house lords can produce more than one positive yoga, thus further elevating prospects for personal success, wealth or other desirable attributes.

By the same token, consider the *Dainya Parivartana Yogas*, with an exchange involving a *trik* lord (eg, lord of the 6th) with the lord of any other house. However, if we restrict our focus, we see that:

- Exchange of the 6th lord with either the 8th or the 12th lords is also a *Viparita Yoga*, suggesting reversal of misfortune.

- This example shows that certain exchanges of house lords can simultaneously produce both a positive and negative yoga, potentially modifying the negative *Dainya Yoga* to a "success after tribulation" scenario as expected under the *Viparita* umbrella.

Aside from forming additional yogas on their own, by virtue of the houses they exchange, one or the other of the planetary pair in a *Parivartana Yoga* can also be in *sambandha* with a third or fourth planet with which it forms yet another yoga.

Obviously, certain yogas will be readily visible when viewed in the planets' natural (pre-exchange) state. But as discussed earlier, the latent power of the *Parivartana Yoga* lies in its participants' potential to be viewed in their post-exchange state as well. However, we are not looking for post-exchange yogas, but for virtual interactions that might affect the *avasthas* (eg, combustion, planetary war) of the post-exchange planet.

Before discussing these other yogas in which the *Parivartana* pair are sometimes engaged, let's make a few distinctions about the formation of yogas. Some are formed only by certain planets, eg, the five true planets for *Pancha Maha Purusha Yoga*, the Moon and Mars for *Chandra Mangala Yoga*, the Moon and Jupiter for *Kesari Yoga*, the Sun and Mercury for *Budhaditya Yoga*, and so on.

Although the nodes don't own any signs to facilitate the house exchange required of *Parivartana Yoga*, they sometimes align with one of the *Parivartana's* players to form node-specific yogas like *Kala Sarpa Yoga* and *Guruchandala Yoga*.

In considering other yogas that could co-exist with *Parivartana*, I've focused less on planet- and node-specific yogas and more on those that are based on house rulership. *Parivartana Yoga* itself hinges on house occupancy and lordship, so my preference is to concentrate on yogas formed by these same house lords.

Following are the additional major yogas typically formed by a *Parivartana* pair as a consequence of house rulership:

- *Dharma Karma Adhipati Yoga*
- *Raja Yoga*
- *Dhana Yoga*
- *Viparita Yoga*

Complete definitions of these yogas are found in Appendix 2.

Yoga vichara

In *yoga vichara* (analysis) we study the participating planets of all yogas to note which houses they occupy, which houses they rule, and the relative strength of each planet. As discussed above, any assessment of planetary strength or weakness requires us to examine their *avasthas*.

Consideration of the *avasthas* can reveal a world of difference between even the most common yogas. For example, *Chandra Mangala Yoga* is formed by either the association or mutual aspect of the Moon and Mars. In a lunar cycle, this happens in two signs out of 12. Therefore, one in six people has a *Chandra Mangala Yoga*.

The Moon and Mars could associate in any sign. The Moon could rotate through the signs, with Mars opposing. Thus, there are 24 distinct combinations for *Chandra Mangala Yoga*.

Are they all equal?

Let's consider the possibilities for association:

1. Moon/Mars conjunct in Aries (Moon ordinary, Mars in its own)
2. Moon/Mars conjunct in Taurus (Moon exalted, Mars ordinary)
3. Moon/Mars conjunct in Cancer (Moon in its own, Mars debilitated)
4. Moon/Mars conjunct in Scorpio (Moon debilitated, Mars in its own)
5. Moon/Mars conjunct in Capricorn (Moon ordinary, Mars exalted)
6. Moon/Mars conjunct in any other sign (Moon and Mars ordinary)

Of the above, numbers 1-2-5 are strongest because their "team" exhibits strength without weakness. Numbers 3-4 are intermediate because their team exhibits both strength and weakness. The other seven combos included in #6 are lackluster because they exhibit no strength.

And, for example, a few of the potential oppositions:

1. Moon in Taurus, Mars in Scorpio (Moon exalted, Mars in its own)
2. Moon in Cancer, Mars in Capricorn (Moon in its own, Mars exalted)
3. Moon in Scorpio, Mars in Taurus (Moon debilitated, Mars ordinary)
4. Moon in Capricorn, Mars in Cancer (Moon ordinary, Mars debilitated)

Among these, the first two are tied in strength, while the second two are tied in weakness. The other eight combinations not listed here offer one strong/ordinary, and the rest just plain ordinary/ordinary.

Our analysis of *Chandra Mangala Yogas* could be extended even further by throwing other variables (including planets) into the mix to create situations of eclipse, new moon, full moon, combustion, planetary war, retrogression of Mars and *dig bala*.

What's the point? Merely to demonstrate that *yoga vichara* has the capacity to make great distinctions between yogas of the same class.

With *Parivartana Yogas*, however, such analysis is inherently more complicated because of the mobility of the two planets involved. Effectively, we must assess the before-and-after situation for each exchange.

By definition, each of the two planets will move to a post-exchange state of *svastha (swa)* – its own sign. But in its pre-exchange state, it occupies another sign in which its *avastha* could be positive, negative, mixed or neutral.

Even after switching the two planets in our minds, however, we must also re-examine the new state of affairs to determine whether combustion, planetary war or eclipse might now plague one of the planetary pair.

Parivartana Yoga's psychological effect

The *Parivartana Yoga* is unique among yogas in its capacity to "psychologize" its effects, as opposed to manifesting them only in a mundane way. In other words, it affords us an opportunity to understand the inner tension of the individual (the "why") in addition to the outer actions and circumstances (the "how") that such a psychological state attracts into the person's life.

Keep in mind that this inner tension may or may not be resolved, depending on the planets involved and what their overall *avasthas* suggest as an outlet or, alternatively, an impasse. More subtly, the person himself may not be consciously aware of or able to articulate this inner tension. Yet it will be the role of the *jyotishi*, not only to identify "where it hurts" but also to recommend a viable resolution.

When one of the pair is initially compromised by debilitation, combustion, planetary war or eclipse, but subsequently moves to its own sign without any complications, that planet is potentially a source of improvement in the native's life. Conversely, when a planet exchanges a neutral situation for a mixed one, eg, *svastha* coexistent with some negative *avastha*, then we shouldn't expect such a stellar outcome.

Aside from its own *avastha*, a planet's participation in other pre-exchange yogas is further indication of its capacity to create the tension inherent in the *Parivartana Yoga*. However, we do not examine the post-exchange state for virtual yogas, but simply for relationships with other planets that might affect the exchange planet's *avasthas*, which in turn is another measure of its potential to resolve that same tension.

Ultimately, it's the symbolic oscillation between sign/house positions that creates a reciprocal tension between the participant planets of a *Parivartana Yoga*. Further, this tension will ultimately be resolved by the planet that enjoys the best of both worlds, as opposed to the planet that achieves basic security in the post-exchange state of *svastha* but suffers in all other regards, whether pre- or post-exchange.

Consider Mars in Capricorn and Saturn in Aries. Mars will oscillate between exaltation and its own sign, while Saturn oscillates between debilitation and its own sign. All other things being equal, Mars will function as the more robust of the pair, and swing the *Parivartana Yoga* in the direction of its house occupation, rulership, and natural significations.

For example, an exchange of 4th and 7th lords may invoke issues related to security and partnerships. Psychologically, this suggests a person whose emotional happiness may have been made vulnerable by an unstable relationship with the mother. Such a psychological imprint might then manifest in multiple ways. The person may form attachments to partners who are distant or always traveling. Or experience domestic problems when a prospective partner enters their personal space. Either situation echoes to some degree the issues of emotional security vis-à-vis a significant nurturing other.

An exchange between 7th and 10th houses may arouse issues related to career and partnerships. Psychologically, the person may have been conditioned by authority figures to believe that a supportive partner is critical to achieving a successful career. This could play out as seeking status through relationships, accepting only suitors who meet the standards of income or power, meanwhile rejecting those with other desirable but less socially-visible qualities. Whether we project our ambitions onto our partners, or pursue our own careers at the risk of our relationships, depends upon the overall *avasthas* of the participant planets.

A *Parivartana Yoga* acts like an irritating grain of sand beneath an oyster's tender mantle. It is an *agent provocateur*, one of the *samskaras* of this particular birth. In order to integrate it, the oyster exudes an inner essence, or *rasa*, until the grain is completely enveloped. Only when this particle of grit has been transformed into a pearl is the oyster ready to offer its beauty to the world.

The degree of irritation caused by the *Parivartana Yoga* is measured by the pre-exchange *avasthas* of its participant planets. The potential quality of the pearl is measured by their post-exchange *avasthas*. So long as no other grit is involved, integration may be reasonably clean. The more grit that enters the picture, however, the greater is its potential to compound the irritation, and thus compromise the integration.

In the first scenario, the individual performs psychological alchemy, resolves their inner tensions, and gives birth to their pearl. But in the second scenario, the person encounters more complications than he has "juice" to deal with, and is unable to resolve the demands of his inner *daemon*. As a consequence, he may spend a lifetime in a revolving door of psychological impulses that manifest as problematic tensions in the areas of life suggested by the weaker of the two planets exchanged.

Control planets

Most *Parivartana Yogas* have a "control planet", ie, one with the capacity to resolve the inherent tension of the exchange, and to swing the resultant outcomes in its favor.

Within every exchange, generally one planet is stronger than the other, no matter whether we view it as absolute or relative strength. Consider a street fight. I'm a normally fit man, but if I face off with a 30-year-old champion of any martial art, he'll beat me because he operates from a position of *absolute* strength. But if I pick a fight with an octogenarian, I'll probably win, because I operate from a position of *relative* strength, ie, I'm ordinary, but he's relatively weaker.

So, within any *Parivartana Yoga*, we can have multiple scenarios with planets that are strong, weak, mixed and ordinary. Determining the appropriate control planet is sometimes straightforward, sometimes complicated, sometimes impossible...

Following is a *pro forma* to determine the control planet for any given pair in an exchange. Although context is everything, these factors are presented in descending order of importance.

1. Compare the primary dignities of each planet: (+) rulership, exaltation, retrogression, *dig bala*, full moon, (-) debilitation, combustion, planetary war, new or eclipsed moon. Remember that some planets can be of mixed condition, ie, both strong/weak, eg, a full Moon in Scorpio.

2. If the two planets are ordinary, or tied for strength, or tied for weakness, consider their involvement in other yogas (pre-exchange only) as a measure of their importance in the chart.

3. If they're still tied for control, compare other factors: (a) whether they are associated with or aspected by the ascendant lord or the Moon, (b) whether they are stabilized by benefics or destabilized by malefics.

On occasion, we'll encounter situations where neither planet enjoys a decisive quality to make it the control planet. In such cases, where nothing exists to break the apparent tie, the exchange pair will operate as coequals within the context of that yoga.

The *gestalt* of *Parivartana Yoga*

Given the various examples presented earlier, we see that planets can exist in different states – positive, negative or neutral – before and after their exchange. The system of dignities provides the primary lens through which we can view the participating planets, and thereby judge with discretion the *gestalt* of the exchange itself.

In summary, we should analyze *Parivartana Yogas* with four considerations in mind:

1. the houses occupied by the participant planets, since these will indicate the primary themes invoked by the yoga,

2. the *avasthas* of the participant planets, before and after exchange, whose evaluation will identify the "control" planet most likely to resolve the tensions created by the yoga,

3. the presence and condition of other planets in the exchange houses, to determine the magnitude and nature of their influence on the outcome of the yoga, and

4. the respective degree positions of the participant planets, whose "range of influence" will determine their potential to interact intimately with other planets and yogas in the chart.

These guidelines will hopefully provide the reader some indication of how to interpret *Parivartana Yogas*. As in much of *Jyotisha*, the perennial challenge is to add nuance and detail to a basic premise. Ultimately, this rests upon our ability to view the situation from different perspectives until, like a hologram, the light of our perception produces a faithful image of reality.

PART 2:

INTERPRETING *PARIVARTANA YOGAS* IN THE CHART

Following are interpretations of the 66 *Parivartana Yoga* combinations. These are based upon, and extrapolated from, brief statements found in *Brihat Parashara Hora Shastra*, Chapter 26, Effects of the Bhava Lords. Thus, each interpretation is prefaced by two pertinent quotations from BPHS: for example, (1) lord of the first in the second, and (2) lord of the second in the first. Whereas the first quote may suggest one outcome, and the second another, the expanded interpretation that follows is a combination of both.

I've also referred to G.S. Agarwal's *Practical Vedic Astrology*, whose succinct comments on *Parivartana Yogas* were literally one-liners. After that, I simply fleshed out expanded statements using other ideas from authors cited in the bibliography, comments made by teachers, and my own interpretation.

Under each *Parivartana Yoga*, you'll find:

- two quotes from BPHS re lords in reciprocal houses,
- a descriptive interpretation of each exchange,
- famous people whose charts have that PVY combo,
- a biography of one famous person with that combo,
- the *rasi* chart for that person, and
- an analysis of that person's *Parivartana Yoga*.

The birth data for all charts used is provided in the List of Case Studies at the end of this book. My original source data was AstroDataBank (now hosted by Astrodienst), whose compilation was based upon work originated by Lois Rodden. In these examples I've included only charts whose birth data met the "AA" or "A" rating in the Rodden system: AA for accurate data as recorded by family or state, A for accurate data as quoted by the person, kin, friend or associate.

Although I've tried to select the best examples, please note that, *no individual life will perfectly epitomize the mutual reception in question*. In other words, we shouldn't expect a mutual reception to describe a whole life; in fact, it will only represent a facet of that life. There are many other astrological factors in play – including other astrological patterns formed by the same planetary pair. Hopefully, the examples offered will illustrate some of the key principles attributed to each mutual reception.

Exchanges Involving the 1st House Lord

Exchange of 1st and 2nd lords

Parashara says:

- *When the lord of the Ascendant has been placed in the 2nd house, the native will be gainful, learned, happy, good-natured, religious-minded, honorable, and will have many wives and good qualities.* (Brihat Parashara Hora Shastra, Chapter 26: Sloka 2)

- *When the 2nd lord has gone in the Ascendant, the native will be endowed with sons and wealth, will be inimical to his family, lustful, hard-hearted and will do other's jobs.* (BPHS 26:13)

This is a *Maha Parivartana Yoga* (also a *Dhana Yoga*) whose lords are in a mutual 2/12 relationship. Because it's a yoga formed with positive-house lords, we expect it to be generally positive in the realm of all things associated with the second house – family and diet, speech and vision, wealth and knowledge.

So the native has a good character: intelligent, upholding family values, strong-willed, passionate, and demonstrating good behavior. He is close to his family, and benefits both materially and intellectually from his association with immediate relatives. He has good study habits, is articulate, has a facility for languages, and a good voice for speaking or singing. Possessing a good vocabulary, he has command of his language, such as would a teacher or a writer.

He enjoys good food, perhaps more than he should, such that either his teeth or his weight reflect his indulgences. He has good vision, both physical eyesight and foresight (both right eye associations), and is a good observer and logician, such that he can make successful plans for the future.

In money matters, he's a natural, and is skilled in accumulating and managing liquid assets. He benefits through family business or profession, with less effort than his peers, and is generous in making gifts to family members and charities. He is knowledgeable in his field and can exchange expertise for income.

Famous people with this yoga

Margery Allingham, mystery writer; Andrea Bocelli, opera singer; Marlon Brando, actor; Richard Branson, entrepreneur; Leo Buscaglia, psychologist; Claudia Cardinale, actress; Rosemary Clooney, singer; David Coulthard, race car driver; Bobby Darin, singer; Alain Delon, actor; Jim Densmore, musician; Dionne quintuplets; Linda Evans, actress; Ché Guevara, revolutionary; Robert Graves, writer; Mohan Koparkar, astrologer; Bob Mackie, fashion designer; Katherine Mansfield, writer; Van Morrison, musician; Joyce Carol Oates, writer; Vance Packard, writer; Arthur Rimbaud, poet; Ernst Roehm, Nazi; Joseph Salk, scientist; Sam Waterston, actor; Bill Wilson, founder of AA.

Case study

Arthur Rimbaud, the precocious French boy-poet of the Symbolist movement, revolutionized poetic language of the time via his use of free verse. He subsequently inspired the Surrealists and many writers of our own age. He was a brilliant student, and considered by his teachers to be a child prodigy. At school he studied Greek and Latin, excelled in rhetoric, and began writing serious poetry, in both French and Latin, by the age of 13, only to completely abandon writing before the age of 21.

Disenchanted by home life, he ran away several times, and took up a homosexual relationship with the poet Paul Verlaine. Both famous and infamous by age 18, he thumbed his nose at the Parisian establishment and cultivated a complete derangement of the senses via absinthe and hashish.

He was known as a libertine and a restless soul, an archetypal *enfant terrible*. A willing expatriate many times over, he learned English, Russian and Arabic in his many travels throughout Europe, and to Indonesia, Yemen and Ethiopia. He died in great pain of bone cancer at age 37.

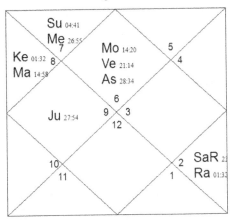

Debilitated Venus in 1st house Virgo exchanges with Mercury in 2nd house Libra. Post-exchange, Mercury gains *dig bala*. Neither planet is subject to combustion.

Before and after exchange, Mercury and Venus associate with weak luminaries. As *karaka* of fathers, the Sun is debilitated; as *karaka* of mothers, the Moon is dark and waning. Thus, this mutual reception also invokes family problems, in part because the exchange planets are in a 2/12 relationship. Rimbaud's father deserted the family when Rimbaud was very young; his mother was severe, prompting him to run away several times.

Since both Mercury and Venus are *rajasik*, there's a certain pitch of activity in 2nd house affairs. His writing was highly inspired, experimental, and hallucinatory, while his drinking and drug consumption contributed to the shaky state of his finances.

On the positive side, the association of Venus and the Moon in mutual *kendras* is a signature of an artist. Venus also participates by association in the *Kesari Yoga* formed by the Moon and Jupiter in *kendras*, which gave Rimbaud his highly adventurous spirit, taking him in travels across Europe and into North Africa.

Since Mercury is ordinary while Venus is debilitated, this gives Mercury the relative strength to function as control planet for this exchange. Its occupation of the 2nd inclined Rimbaud to substance abuse, linguistics and writing.

Exchange of 1st and 3rd lords

Parashara says:

- *Should the Ascendant lord be placed in the 3rd house, the native will be equal to a lion in valor, will have all kinds of wealth, will be honorable, will have two wives, and be intelligent and happy.* (BPHS 26:3)

- *Should the 3rd lord be situated in the Ascendant, the native will have self-made wealth, will be disposed to serve, valorous and intelligent, although devoid of learning.* (BPHS 26:25)

This is a *Khala Parivartana Yoga* whose lords are in a mutual 3/11 relationship. As a yoga including a mild *dusthana* lord, we expect it to have an "alternating current" effect, giving as many problems as benefits.

Involving the 1st and 3rd lords, we get a sense of personal (mis)adventures, based perhaps on some inherent character or physical flaw, and finding expression via the arts, sports or some other activity that demands dexterity or skill.

The native has a somewhat dubious or shifty character: sometimes polite, other times speaking harshly of others. Generally unsteady of mind, he has trouble concentrating for any lengthy period of time. Because he is inclined to seek adventures, he thinks a lot about sex, is inclined to wander, and may therefore pursue more than one relationship at a time.

Siblings are a focal element in his family life, and he may have one among them who is near and dear to his heart, somewhat like a best friend. Because of the 3/11 relationship of the lords, his younger siblings enjoy gains or profits.

His courage waxes and wanes – bold on one occasion, timid on another. Frequently challenged and troubled by competition, his efforts in life are inconsistent. Because of frequent failures, he may develop a do-or-die attitude toward his ambitions. Sometimes foolhardy, he endures physical risks, suffering injuries to the neck, shoulder or arms. Because of his strenuous physical activities, he may eat more than others.

He has special talents in sports or the arts, especially in fields that require significant physical dexterity or adroitness.

Famous people with this yoga

George W. Bush, US President; Bob Crane, actor; Robert Desnos, surrealist; Zipporah Dobyns, astrologer; Jane Fonda, actress; Tama Janowitz, writer; Diane Keaton, actress; Evel Knievel, daredevil; Sugar Ray Leonard, boxer; Bette Bao Lord, writer; Michael Milken, investor; Pele, soccer player; Saint Teresa of Avila, religious icon; Liz Smith, gossip columnist; Richie Valens, singer; Mike Wallace, TV personality; Dwight Yoakam, singer.

Case study

Evel Knievel, the hell-raising stuntman who rode his motorcycle to daredevil fame, has been an active athlete in many sports throughout his life, eg, skier, pole vaulter, hockey player. After leaving high school he got a job at a local mine but was fired after he performed a "wheelie" with a large earth-moving vehicle and crashed into a power line. As a young man, he launched an environmental protest campaign to protect elk in national parks, a form of penance after he'd been discovered guiding deer-hunting trips in Yellowstone National Park. For awhile, he was an insurance salesman and ran a Honda dealership at which he offered $100 discounts for any customer who could beat him arm-wrestling.

He's a veteran of multiple stunt injuries (75 ramp-to-ramp motorcycle jumps) that have resulted in 433 fractures in 35 bones, thus earning him a spot in the *Guinness Book of World Records* as the survivor of "most bones broken in a lifetime." In getting repaired, he's endured no fewer than 14 operations, during one of which he contracted hepatitis C, and was obliged to have a liver transplant!

With a past as checkered as his medical record, Knievel has been arrested for various acts of violence – assaulting his girlfriend, sexually soliciting an undercover cop, and beating his press agent with a baseball bat, a rules infraction that earned him six months in jail.

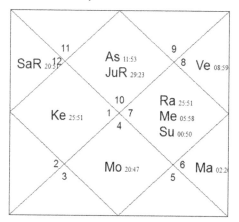

Debilitated Jupiter in 1st house Capricorn exchanges with Saturn in 3rd house Pisces. The two planets are both retrograde and therefore strong. Given Jupiter's role as *karaka* for the liver, its debilitation is suggestive both of his hepatitis and the subsequent transplant of organs. Jupiter is in a *Kesari*

Yoga with a strong Moon, giving him public fame. Although Jupiter escapes debilitation to become *swa* in the exchange, it loses *dig bala* in the process and is thereby somewhat compromised. Call it impaired judgment leading to rash actions.

Lagnesh Saturn in the 3rd is aspected by Mars, giving both a *Dharma Karma Adhipati* and a *Dhana Yoga*. However, with two malefic and *tamasik* planets, this perhaps explains his aggressive streak, his dogged defiance in the face of danger, and the multiple accidents that have earned him so many broken bones.

Since Jupiter is debilitated while Saturn is ordinary, this gives Saturn the relative strength to function as control planet for this exchange. Its placement in the 3rd gave Knievel a love of risky adventures.

Exchange of 1st and 4th lords

Parashara says:

- *Should the Ascendant lord be in the 4th house, the native will be blessed with paternal and maternal happiness, many brothers, and will be lascivious, virtuous and charming.* (BPHS 26:4)

- *When the 4th lord is situated in the Ascendant, the native is blessed with learning, virtues, ornaments, lands, conveyances and maternal happiness.* (BPHS 26:37)

This is a *Maha Parivartana Yoga* (also a *Dharma Karma Adhipati Yoga*) whose lords are in a mutual 4/10 relationship from *kendra* houses. As a yoga formed via positive house lords, we anticipate good results, and with angularity, visible results.

Engaging the 1st and 4th lords, we expect a strong personality or some charisma to play a role in achieving something notable in 4th house themes, such as psychology, education, community, or property.

The native has a stable and dynamic character, a strong sense of morals, and loyalty for things associated with his ancestry, domestic environment and country. He is fond of his mother, with whom he shares physical or personality characteristics, and whose values he respects. She has a good profession, reputation or status, and is a significant influence on his character.

His education is solid, in a field related to earth sciences, psychology or teaching. He is attached to his home and takes pride in his property, vehicles and major possessions. He tends to accumulate fixed assets. He might well be a loyalist, a patriot or a nationalist, insofar as it concerns his civic community, political allegiances or country.

His happiness is linked to his physical well-being. He pays a lot of attention to physical fitness and health, clothes and personal attractiveness. Happiness of the body implies sexual enjoyments, which leads him to seek sexual experience as a source of happiness. Having achieved his own satisfaction, he may further address his activities to making others happy, especially those that could be considered part of his community or constituency.

Famous people with this yoga

Joe Adonis, Mafia boss; Robert Altman, producer; Shirley Temple Black, actress; Jeff Bridges, actor; Joe Cocker, singer; Billy Crystal, comedian; Samantha Fox, actress; Nancy Hastings, astrologer; Henri Landru, serial killer; Maria Montessori, educator; Rod Stewart, singer; Sigourney Weaver, actress; Tennessee Williams, playwright.

Case study

Maria Montessori, founder of the renowned educational system and school network that bears her name, was the first woman in Italy to receive a medical degree, despite hostility from male colleagues during her studies.

Although she had a child after an affair with a fellow doctor, she declined to marry because she didn't want to resign her position. Instead, she placed her son in foster care until he was a teenager, after which he became an assistant in her research.

During her medical work in orphanages, hospitals and asylums, she became concerned about the low level of scholastic ability in the children she encountered. With no formal training in education *per se*, she got involved in the schooling of children.

One of her key insights was that environment had a huge effect on learning. Following this revelation, she subsequently evolved a unique method of teaching, an educational methodology that has since been exported around the world. Young students learned through activities involving exploration, manipulations, order, repetition, abstraction, and communication, before later moving on to reasoning, imagination, and creativity.

She became a public advocate for children's education before founding the *Casa dei Bambini* schools that formed the model of the network that ultimately went international.

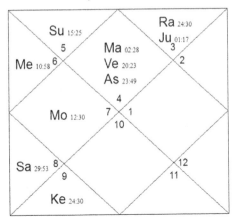

Venus in 1st house Cancer exchanges with the Moon in 4th house Libra. *Lagnesh* Moon obtains strength pre-exchange via *dig bala* in the 4th, while Venus achieves *dig bala* post-exchange, thus reinforcing the theme of education via the exchange of these two natural benefics.

Venus with a debilitated Mars in the ascendant creates two *Dharma Karma Adhipati Yogas.* The pair is hemmed by malefics Sun and Rahu to form a *Papa Kartari Yoga* that suggests her scientific training, as well as the many obstacles she faced in her profession. The combination of Venus and the Moon in *kendras* is also a signature of an artist, and although Montessori did not follow this particular career path, one of the main tenets of her philosophy was that environment (architecture and interior decorating) both had a substantial influence on learning outcomes.

Since both exchange planets are ordinary, neither seems a candidate for control planet. If forced to choose, however, the association of Venus with a debilitated Mars diminishes its status. This arguably makes the Moon the control planet for this exchange. Its placement in the 4th house evokes the system of education for which she became renowned.

Exchange of 1st and 5th lords

Parashara says:

- *In case the Ascendant lord has gone into the 5th house, the native will have mediocre happiness through his sons, the first born will not live; he will be honorable, wrathful and favorite to a king.* (BPHS 26:5)

- *Should the 5th lord occupy the Ascendant, the native will be scholarly, be blessed with progenic happiness, be miserly, crooked, and a stealer of other's wealth.* (BPHS 26:49)

This is a *Maha Parivartana Yoga* (also a *Raja Yoga*) wherein the lords are in a mutual 5/9 relationship from *trikona* houses. An exchange of (positive) *dharma* house lords suggests benefits of *purva punya*, or good karma from previous lives. Involving houses that represent the *atma* (Self), *ahamkara* (ego) and *buddhi* (discriminating mind), we anticipate a substantial personal, intellectual or spiritual experience.

As a consequence, the native has an intellectual disposition, good intelligence and a facility for both learning and teaching. He enjoys good karma (*purva punya*) from the virtuous deeds of his previous life, the fruit of which is manifested in the quality of his mind, his creativity, and the nature of his children.

His mind is alert, concentrated and aware. Within his circle, he is respected for his intelligence. Because he is spiritually inclined, his thoughts turn naturally to prayers, positive visualizations and mantras for improvement.

His children display good intelligence. He delights in telling them stories, both fanciful and true. His children are obedient, and he in turn respects their opinions, such that in time he falls under their influence. His children pursue higher studies in combination with foreign travel.

He enjoys success in government and politics. He is also lucky in gambling and speculation, especially related to sports.

Famous people with this yoga

Karl Barth, theologian; Carol Channing, actress; Tim Curry, actor; John Flamsteed, astronomer; Paul René Fonck, WW1 ace pilot; Peter Frampton, musician; Ulysses S. Grant, US President; Alex Haley, writer; Stephen King, writer; Lynne Palmer, astrologer; Algernon Swinburne, poet; Dennis Wheatley, occult author; Steve Winwood, musician; Michael York, actor.

Case study

Stephen King, one of the most commercially successful writers of all time, has proven himself both prolific and astute when it comes to knowing what fears lurk beneath the beds of America. His 54 horror fiction novels have sold more than 350 million copies, many of which have been adapted into feature films, miniseries, television shows and comic books. He has received multiple awards for his writing.

Although incredibly successful in his professional life, King has had his personal misfortunes. Years after overcoming substance addiction, he was struck by a van while walking on the road near his home. The crippling accident sidelined him for months, principally from a broken hip and a right leg so shattered that doctors initially considered amputating his leg.

King is politically vocal, speaking out on behalf of Democrats and against Republicans, particularly the Tea Party. He donates roughly $4 million to charities. He stands at the center of a writing family. His wife Tabitha has published nine novels, and their two sons have both published short story collections. King loves hard rock music, which plays in the background while he writes, and is a big fan of the Boston Red Sox.

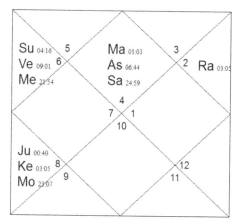

Mars in 1st house Cancer exchanges with the Moon in 5th house Scorpio. Both are debilitated, and gain doubly by resuming their own signs. With both ascendant lord and occupant debilitated, we expect some dysfunctionality. To his credit, King admitted to years of alcohol and cocaine abuse. Equally to his credit (and perhaps the redemptive power of his *Parivartana Yoga*), he pulled himself back from self-destruction in time to continue his stellar career.

Mars and Saturn in the 1st form two *Dharma Karma Adhipati Yogas*, a saving grace in light of these two prime malefics joining forces in his *lagna*. Suffice to say, King must have teetered on the dark edge more than once. No wonder he wrote such darkly macabre material.

The Moon with Jupiter in the 5th forms both a *Dharma Karma Adhipati* and *Kesari Yoga*, albeit afflicted by the Rahu-Ketu axis. A brilliant, creepy mind (5th) is only one manifestation of the exchange. Physical (1st) problems are also likely, eg, the substance abuse now under control, the near-fatal accident with a runaway vehicle, and the ongoing potential for blood/liver disorders. Since the Moon and Mars are mutual friends, we get a sense that the exchange will work out, particularly on a mental/spiritual plane, and in relations with his children, all being invoked via the 5th house.

Since Mars is associated with its enemy Saturn, while the Moon is with its friend Jupiter, this suggests the Moon as the appropriate control planet in this exchange. Its placement in the 5th house of creative self-expression speaks to his prolific career as a writer.

Exchange of 1st and 6th lords

Parashara says:

- *In the event of the Ascendant lord having fallen in the 6th house, the native is deprived of bodily pleasures. If the Ascendant lord is under the influence of a malefic and has no benefic aspect on him, he will be troubled by an enemy.* (BPHS 26:6)

- *If the 6th lord is situated in the Ascendant, the native will be sickly, famous, inimical to his relatives, adventurous and virtuous.* (BPHS 26:61)

This is a *Dainya Parivartana Yoga* wherein the lords are in a mutual 6/8 relationship. Because the exchange involves a *trik* lord, we expect mostly difficulties, although since the 6th is also an *upachaya* house, things can improve through time and effort.

The native has a contentious character, and is both brave and jealous. He hoards money. Eager to compete, and intent on constant malevolence, he gets involved in litigation and other conflicts. He creates obstacles for his enemies.

His health is good, the result of either a strong constitution free from disease, a powerful physique developed through sports, or a resistance to illness built up via frequent minor ailments.

He makes enemies as easily as others make friends, both in his place of employment and in his family circle. Of the latter, he enjoys a special love/hate relationship with his mother's siblings, who experience hardships, illness or danger in their lives.

Very much a realist, not a daydreamer, he works hard for a living, and takes special pride in physical labor. Drawn to fields such as medicine, police, and the military, he shares a special affinity with animals, either as pets, or through veterinary work.

Famous people with this yoga

Sri Aurobindu, spiritual leader; Eddie Albert, actor; Milton Berle, comedian; Sandra Bernhard, comedienne; Kenneth Branagh, actor; Natalie Cole, singer; Morgan Fairchild, actress; Federico Fellini, director; Edouard Manet, artist; Marie Antoinette, Queen of France; Julianne Moore, actress; Jackie Robinson, baseball player; Mark Spitz, Olympic swimmer; Algernon Swinburne, poet; Penny Thornton, astrologer; Robert Zoller, astrologer.

Case study

Edouard Manet, an artist of the 19th Century whose name is almost synonymous with the Impressionist movement, started out to pursue a naval career, but after a year as a sea cadet, flunked his naval exams and decided to become an artist instead. Extremely prolific, with a catalog of over 400 works, he defied artistic conventions of the day by using beggars, prostitutes and common Parisians as his subjects, and rendering them in a bold rough style that contrasted with the detailed work of his contemporaries.

Without seeking controversy, he was labeled a radical painter, and vilified by the art establishment for his treatment of certain subjects. During the Franco-Prussian War, he served as a gunner in the National Guard, before resuming his place at the center of an Impressionist group that included Degas, Renoir and Monet, the latter's name being so similar as to cause confusion for the public, and great irritation to Monet.

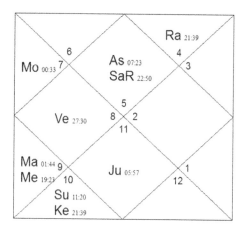

Saturn in 1st house Leo exchanges with the Sun in 6th house Capricorn. This is an exchange of malefics who are mutual enemies. The 6th house themes were manifested in multiple ways: his uncle's influence in developing his artistic taste and technical bias; his stints in both the merchant marine and the National Guard; the fierce public criticism of his "bohemian" work; and even his competition with Monet for the name most identified with Impressionism.

His strong (retrograde) Saturn is involved in a *Dharma Karma Adhipati Yoga* via the mutual aspect with Jupiter. Assisted perhaps by the power of this yoga, Manet became a ground-breaking influence for the Impressionist movement via his technical innovations, and shared acclaim in conjunction with notoriety. Since *lagnesh* Sun is tainted by association with the Rahu-Ketu axis, Manet's health ultimately suffered, and he died from gangrene, despite the amputation of a leg.

Since the Sun is ordinary and afflicted by the nodal axis while Saturn is retrograde and stabilized by Jupiter, this acknowledges Saturn as the appropriate control planet. Its position in the ascendant speaks to his hard-won fame and his many physical struggles.

Exchange of 1st and 7th lords

Parashara says:

- *If the Ascendant lord is a malefic and he occupies the 7th house, the native's wife will not live. If the Ascendant lord is a benefic planet, the native is an aimless wanderer, penurious, of ascetic disposition, or becomes a king.* (BPHS 26:7)

- *In case the 7th lord happens to fall in the Ascendant, the native will traverse other people's wives, be wicked, skillful, be devoid of fortitude, and will be afflicted by windy diseases.* (BPHS 26:73)

This is a *Maha Parivartana Yoga* (also a *Dharma Karma Adhipati Yoga*) wherein the lords are in a 7/7 relationship from *kendra* houses. This *sambandha* serves to strengthen each other's significations (the Self and the Other), and would typically be made public due to the angularity of the two participants.

Because of this dynamic, ie, a literal opposition between the 1st and 7th lords, we expect this yoga to strongly manifest in the arena of relationships, whether personal, social or professional.

The native has an amorous disposition, and is interested in the spouses of others. Tantalized by desire, he finds it difficult to settle with one partner, such that he is bound to an endless cycle of attraction and repulsion, union and separation. His life may thus be a carousel of partners, such that it signifies a major theme of his life.

His inclination for relationship-building will also play out in a professional context, eg, through fields such as customer relations, sales and marketing, public relations, performance art or international diplomacy. Effectively, the person becomes an agent of some kind or other.

He is interested in travel, partly for business, but mostly due to a profound restlessness that makes him wander endlessly.

Famous people with this yoga

Giulio Andreotti, politician; Rupert Brooke, poet; Rick Danko, musician; Doris Day, actress; John Denver, singer; Indira Gandhi, politician; James Earl Jones, actor; Shirley MacLaine, actress; Maximilian I, German Emperor; Susan Sarandon, actress; Robert Stack, actor; Jacqueline Susann, writer.

Case study

Jacqueline Susann, the original and undisputed Queen of Pulp Fiction, is the only writer to have three novels in a row hit #1 on the *New York Times'* bestseller list. A pot-smoking teenager with a reputed IQ of 140 who had a lifelong, warped crush on her philandering father, Susann subsequently failed as an actress, model, singer, and playwright before turning to writing in her 40s. Her enormously devoted husband worked tirelessly to promote her career, in spite of her chronic infidelities with comedians and stars of both sexes, including Eddie Cantor, George Jessel, Ethel Merman and Coco Chanel.

Considered a better schmoozer than a writer, she swore like a trucker, punched agents and critics who crossed her, and once threw a drink at Johnny Carson in a bar. Plagued with insecurities and pain from a mastectomy, she drank and took pills to cope, once attempting suicide by trying to leap from her terrace, after which her husband handcuffed himself to her to prevent further attempts. She loved pets, basing her first book on her poodle, and had one child, a son who was diagnosed autistic and spent his life institutionalized.

~

The Moon in 1st house Capricorn exchanges with Saturn in 7th house Cancer. *Lagnesh* Saturn enjoys *dig bala* in the 7th and thus exerts considerable strength. But pre- or post-exchange, Saturn opposes *Chandralagna*, and because Saturn is naturally obstructive, it takes over as an anti-social or anti-marital influence. This may explain Susann's desperate impulse to try to please everyone, all the while pretending she didn't really give a damn, leading to convoluted relationships.

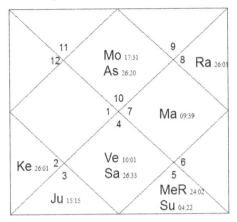

The Moon/Saturn mutual aspect also constitutes a *Dharma Karma Adhipati Yoga*. We get a sense of achievement via partnerships, albeit with considerable friction. The addition of Venus on the Moon/Saturn axis puts an added spin on things, immersing her in dramatic arts, sex, and luxury living.

As lord of the 5th and the 10th, Venus amplifies the Moon/Saturn *Dharma Karma Adhipati Yoga* by adding three more of the same, one with the Moon, and two with *lagnesh* Saturn. Finally, Saturn is embraced by a *Shubhadhi* Yoga involving Jupiter, Venus and Mercury, thus intensifying the relationship themes of her life, via both her promiscuity and her devoted spouse. Note her career breakthrough at age 45, halfway through her Saturn *dasa*, after Saturn had transited her ascendant to cue the yoga into manifestation.

Since the Moon is full, while Saturn has *dig bala*, the choice of control planet is not immediately clear. But the Moon is aspected by two malefics, while Saturn enjoys the association/aspect of two benefics, thus suggesting Saturn's greater influence. Its placement in the 7th reflects her preoccupation with relationships – marital, extra-marital and professional.

Exchange of 1st and 8th lords

Parashara says:

- *Should the Ascendant lord occupy the 8th house, the native will be Siddha Vidya Visharada (having the knowledge of occult powers), sickly, thievish, extremely wrathful, a gambler, and given to traversing other's wives.* (BPHS 26:8)

- *If the 8th lord happens to be placed in the Ascendant, the native will be bereft of bodily pleasures, be detractor of gods and Brahmins, and will have wounds.* (BPHS 26:85)

This is a *Dainya Parivartana Yoga* wherein the lords are in a mutual 6/8 relationship. Because this exchange involves a *trik* lord, who has no virtues other than trial-by-trauma, we expect problems in spades.

The native's character is flawed by nature, such that he is valiant in performing mean acts, and stubborn in doing virtuous acts. He is a gambler, a cheat, and a thug, or associates with people of a similar disposition.

His longevity is good, but he has bad habits that do harm to his health, or place him in physical jeopardy. Therefore, his life is marked by constant mishaps, accidents, traumas and reversals of fortune, such that he is chronically plagued by injuries or disease. His partner's family is also liable to illness, conflict, and litigation.

He is prone to getting into situations of abuse, violence, sexual servitude, or financial mismanagement, especially concerning the money of business or romantic partners.

Curious, he loves mysteries, and is skilled in research and investigation. He has knowledge of occult subjects but is generally disrespectful of traditional religion. This may favor careers requiring stealth, secrecy, extreme measures, and reversal of circumstances.

Famous people with this yoga

Noam Chomsky, philosopher; Glenn Close, actress; Abigail Folger, coffee heiress; Amyr Klynck, adventurer; Buz Myers, astrologer; Ilie Nastase, tennis player; Dinah Shore, entertainer; Sirhan Sirhan, assassin; August Strindberg, writer; Edgar Winter, musician.

Case study

Abigail Folger, heiress to the Folger coffee fortune, studied art history at Harvard and later became active in civil rights and community welfare, doing volunteer work with ghetto children in Los Angeles. Sadly, she gained her 15 minutes of fame by being in the wrong place at the wrong time.

In the spring of 1969, both Roman Polanski and his wife Sharon Tate were away so much on film projects that they asked Folger and her boyfriend to house-sit their LA home. The night of August 8th, when Sharon Tate and another friend were visiting, four members of Charles Manson's cult crashed their party. Along with three other victims, Folger was brutally murdered in a killing spree that shocked America, and put one more nail in the coffin of the hippie era.

Although he had no direct exposure to Folger, Charles Manson was subsequently convicted under the "joint responsibility" rule of law. The murder conspiracy that he'd hatched was intended to ignite an apocalyptic race war he called "Helter Skelter."

~

The Moon in 1st house Sagittarius exchanges with Jupiter in 8th house Cancer. This is an exchange of natural benefics, both of which are *sattvik* planets. *Lagnesh* Jupiter in association with the Sun creates a *Dharma Karma Adhipati Yoga*. Jupiter gives up its exaltation for its own sign, but gains *dig bala* by transference. Post-exchange, if we consider the Moon to assume the same degree position as Jupiter, it (virtually) becomes eclipsed.

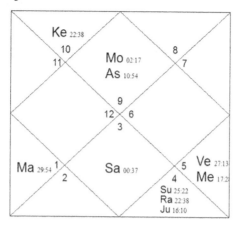

Although the exchange of *sattvik* benefics via the 8th suggests the handsome legacy to which she was heir, both parties to the exchange are damaged. The 8th house occupant is triply afflicted – by the aspect of Mars, association with the Sun, and contamination by the Rahu-Ketu axis. The Moon, which occupies the 1st house, is harmed by the close aspect of a Saturn made powerful via *dig bala*.

Note as well the *Guruchandala Yoga* (Jupiter with Rahu) formed in the 8th house. Although he was certainly not her mentor, Manson's status as a cult leader and the role he played in her death lends credence to the notion that Folger would suffer from a "flawed guru relationship."

Since the Moon is full while Jupiter is exalted, the choice of control planet is not immediately clear. But the Moon is afflicted by only one malefic, while Jupiter is afflicted by three, thus suggesting the Moon's greater influence. Its placement in the 1st reflects the dubious (and ephemeral) fame of a life cut short by tragedy.

Exchange of 1st and 9th lords

Parashara says:

- *If the Ascendant lord is situated in the 9th house, the native will be fortunate, dear to the people, devotee of Lord Vishnu, skillful, eloquent speaker, and will be endowed with wife, sons and wealth.* (BPHS 26:9)

- *If the 9th lord is placed in the Ascendant, the native will be fortunate, prosperous, be honored by the king (or government), good natured, charming, and be honored by the people.* (BPHS 26:97)

This is a *Maha Parivartana Yoga* (also a *Raja Yoga*) wherein the lords are in a mutual 5/9 relationship from *trikona* houses. Since two *dharma* lords are involved, we again get the sense of *punya*, although this time it is good karma generated as a consequence of the current life.

The native has a virtuous character, and is disposed to religious observances and charities. As a consequence, he enjoys the favor of both church and state, and receives some recognition or honors from them.

He is fond of his father, with whom he shares some physical or personality characteristics. If we adopt the perspective of the 9th house, and see the exchange from the 5th house away, we might also assume that the father is an adventurer, a speculator, or one who takes risks.

He creates good karma in his present life, largely through the proper application of his mind, and his devotion to both father and guru. He is dedicated to his spiritual development, and is fortunate in finding a proper guru, whom he serves as his master.

He does well in the fields of law, higher education, publishing and the travel industry. He travels extensively, either for his higher education or for spiritual pilgrimage, and may take up residence in a foreign country.

Famous people with this yoga

Cyd Charisse, dancer; Derek Clayton, track & field star; Christie Hefner, publisher; Erica Jong, writer; Gary Kasparov, chess grandmaster; Jacques Lacan, psychoanalyst; Ricky Martin, singer; Nick Nolte, actor; Franz Schubert, composer; Irving Wallace, writer; Harold Wilson, politician.

Case study

Franz Schubert, the 19th century Austrian composer, left behind more unfinished music than any great composer. He wrote as many as eight songs a day and, by the time he died at age 31, had a colossal lifework of nearly 1,000 compositions, the most famous being the aptly-titled "Unfinished Symphony". The 12th child of a schoolteacher father who inspired him to play music, he studied first under the parish church's choir master, and later under the famous Antonio Salieri, Mozart's teacher. For a time he worked at the same school as his father, played music at church, and composed masses of his own.

Poor and unworldly, he relied on the support of friends but, despite a bohemian lifestyle, always awoke early and composed every day until noon after which he went out drinking. He had a mysterious love life, and probably contracted syphilis from a servant girl. He was subsequently treated with mercury, which left him bald for over a year, and gave him headaches and vertigo until his death. Although he died of "nerve fever", it was more likely due to an occlusion of a cerebral artery resulting from syphilis.

~

Saturn in 1st house Gemini exchanges with Mercury in 9th house Aquarius. Saturn and Mercury are friends, and neuters. *Lagnesh* Mercury associates with a *Kesari Yoga* in the 9th, a combination which further generates two *Dharma Karma Adhipati Yogas* with Jupiter and a *Dhana Yoga* with the Moon.

Saturn in the ascendant, which has first-tier strength via its retrogression, mutually aspects Venus to generate a *Raja Yoga* involving the 5th and 9th lords. The 9th house themes are strongly evident via the influence of his father, the church, and a famous "guru".

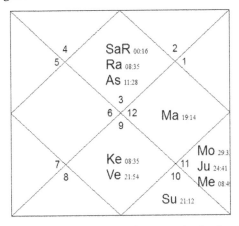

Pre- or post-exchange, Jupiter influences both the 1st and 9th houses and their lords, thus inspiring his enormous productivity.

Post-exchange, Mercury gains *dig bala* in moving to the 1st, but in transferring its own degree position, becomes seriously compromised by close contact with the Rahu-Ketu axis and its *Kala Sarpa Yoga*. Dysfunctional relationships and a lifetime of problematic health, including syphilis and typhoid, were the most obvious manifestations of this, the other being his dubious distinction of having produced so much yet left so much unfinished. For the latter we need look no further than the exchange occurring in his Gemini ascendant, the archetypal sign of distraction.

Whereas Mercury is ordinary, Saturn is retrograde, thus making it the control planet for this exchange. Saturn's placement in the 1st house speaks to both his fame and the great struggles of his life.

Exchange of 1st and 10th lords

Parashara says:

- *Should the Ascendant lord be situated in the 10th house, the native will be endowed with paternal happiness, will enjoy royal favor, fame among men, and will undoubtedly have self-earned wealth.* (BPHS 26:10)

- *Should the 10th lord be situated in the Ascendant, the native will be learned, famous, be a poet, will incur diseases in childhood, be happy later on, and his wealth will increase day by day.* (BPHS 26:109)

This is a *Maha Parivartana Yoga* (also a *Dharma Karma Adhipati Yoga*) wherein the lords are in a mutual 4/10 relationship from *kendra* houses, thus suggesting a bias for visible activity and accomplishment, particularly in the career, and possibly leading to some degree of fame (or notoriety).

The native is of an ambitious nature and material disposition, desiring power, authority, recognition and the accumulation of possessions. He achieves an elevated status and becomes known within his social circle for his wealth and/or his independent profession. He is a self-made man, and enjoys plenty of gains and vehicles. He may enjoy a special relationship with his partner's mother.

With a bias for self-employment or entrepreneurial ventures, he is capable of managing projects with little or no supervision. He is natural management material and, whether through simple desire for power or genuine organizational skills, he is capable of exercising leadership and directing control of large enterprises.

His career involves the physical body or personality in some active way, eg, athlete, model, performer, actor, politician, motivational speaker. He is also interested in aviation, meteorology and astronomy.

Famous people with this yoga

Steve Allen, comedian; Donald Byrd, musician; Francois Duvalier, dictator; José Feliciano, blind musician; Naomi Judd, singer; Ethel Kennedy, political wife; René Jules Lalique, designer; Joan McEvers, astrologer; Marvin Mitchelson, attorney; Don Schollander, Olympic swimmer; David Souter, Supreme Court jurist; Jess Stearn, occult writer.

Case study

Ethel Kennedy, the archetype and living icon of an American matriarchy, was born into wealth as the daughter of a coal magnate whose house was always filled with priests and nuns. Tragedy has been at her elbow throughout her life. Both her alcoholic parents and a brother died in separate plane crashes. Her husband Bobby was assassinated during his Presidential bid campaign. Two of her 11 children died accidentally. Both brothers-in-law suffered tragedy – President John F. Kennedy was assassinated, and Senator Edward Kennedy was implicated in the Chappaquiddick scandal.

In addition, dozens of her extended family were implicated in mysterious and/or fatal circumstances – car accidents, plane crashes, house fires, drug overdoses, skiing mishaps, rapes, accidental shootings, and murders. A devout Catholic whose faith has been tested countless times over the decades, she continues to be a faithful church-goer to this day. Perhaps in penance for a karmic legacy that hovers like a black cloud over the Kennedys, she has been devoted throughout her active life to public service, ranging from domestic housing issues to international medical assistance.

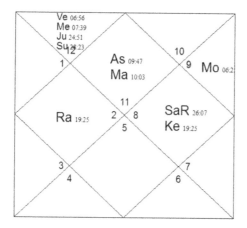

Mars in Aquarius 1st exchanges with Saturn in Scorpio 10th. This is an exchange of natural malefics, with Mars the enemy of Saturn. Mars gains strength via *dig bala* through the exchange, but at the cost of becoming tainted by the *Kala Sarpa* configuration in the 4th/10th axis. Saturn has strength via its retrogression, and both malefics aspect the 7th house. Along with Rahu and Ketu, they dominate the angles and thus the karmic themes of this life.

The sheer number and magnitude of tragedies by which her life has been marked is the signature of a *Kala Sarpa dosha* amplified by the exchange of two malefics. It's interesting to note that, when her husband Bobby was assassinated, she was running the *dasa-bhukti* of Mars-Rahu, while transiting Mars opposed natal Saturn to the exact degree.

Mars is ordinary while Saturn is retrograde and aspected by a strong benefic, thus granting it the role of control planet for this exchange. Its placement in the 10th is symptomatic of private tragedies lived large in the public eye.

Exchange of 1st and 11th lords

Parashara says:

- *In case the Ascendant lord has been placed in the 11th house, the native will always have gains, good qualities, fame and many wives.* (BPHS 26:11)

- *If the 11th lord is placed in the Ascendant, the native will be of Sattwika nature, be rich, happy, even-sighted, a poet, eloquent in speech, and be always endowed with gains.* (BPHS 26:121)

This is a *Maha Parivartana Yoga* (also a *Dhana Yoga*) wherein the lords are in a mutual 3/11 relationship. Because of this configuration, with one of the participants being an *upachaya* house lord, we expect results to be commensurate with personal desire and effort, improving over time.

The native is virtuous, scholarly, patient and persevering. He has a strong constitution and works hard, such that he enjoys a long and productive life. He achieves his hopes and desires, especially in the matter of wealth, which he earns through fair means.

He has a lot of friends, including those of the opposite sex, with whom he forms close relationships. His social circle includes people from business, political and artistic backgrounds. Elder siblings will be near and dear to him, and treated as best friends. Siblings will undertake frequent short journeys.

He is eloquent with words, and could be a writer. He is also adept at handling money. Professionally, he could be a financial advisor, an investment fund manager, a group facilitator, a team-builder, a political bagman, or fundraiser for social causes.

Famous people with this yoga

Queen Beatrix, Dutch royalty; Tony Blair, politician; Bill Blass, designer; Charles Bukowski, writer; M.C. Escher, artist; Martha Graham, dancer; Bobby Knight, basketball coach; Patrick McGoohan, actor; Lord Louis Mountbatten, British royalty; Mort Sahl, entertainer; Ted Turner, entrepreneur; Walt Whitman, poet; Esther Williams, actress & swimmer.

Case study

Charles Bukowski, *bête noire* of American fiction, is best known via the autobiographical portrayal of his lifestyle in the movie *Barfly*. A notorious drinker and womanizer, Bukowski was a prolific poet, short story writer and novelist whose low-life subjects – the drunken, destitute and debauched denizens of the race track, backstreet bars and flophouses of Los Angeles – assured that his work would never be embraced by the mainstream. Although saddled for years with menial jobs, Bukowski ultimately produced over 60 books. Largely ignored in America, he enjoyed enormous appeal in Europe, where both Jean-Paul Sartre and Jean Genet called him "America's greatest poet".

In his youth he suffered from violent beatings from his alcoholic father, and acne so severe that his boils had to be surgically drilled before draining. He married twice and lived with dozens of other women. Decades of heavy drinking rewarded him with a bleeding ulcer that hospitalized and almost killed him. He admired strength and endurance, and largely rejected the goals that most people strive after. Few other writers of the 20th century appeared so willing to shed authorial dignity in the pursuit of grainy truths.

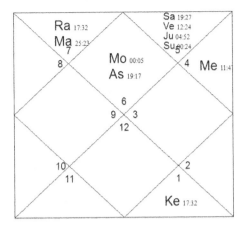

The Moon in 1st house Virgo exchanges with Mercury in 11th house Cancer. In this chart, Mercury is a benefic, but the Moon is so compromised that it fails to retain any positive qualities, being dark, *sandhi* (on the very cusp of a sign) and massively hemmed by four malefics. Post-exchange, Mercury gains *dig bala* while the Moon becomes *swa*. Aside from the malignant *Papa Kartari Yoga* on the ascendant, neither of the two exchange planets is involved in any other yoga.

Only the Moon is in a *kendra*, which explains in part his relative obscurity in mainstream publishing. And reflective perhaps of the four planets in his 12th house (of foreign matters), Bukowski's reputation was much greater overseas than at home, although he allegedly received a flood of fan mail from the insane and incarcerated in America.

Mercury does far better in the exchange than does the Moon. Whereas the Moon remains dark (within three *tithis* of the Sun) no matter whether pre- or post-exchange, Mercury goes from ordinary to twice-dignified. Given this dynamic, we can understand that within one man there could coexist both a consummate writer and a dissolute rogue.

In light of Mercury's relative dominance, this confirms it as the control planet in this exchange. Its placement in the 11th house speaks to his ultimate success as a writer.

Exchange of 1st and 12th lords

Parashara says:

- *In the event of the Ascendant lord being placed in the 12th house, the native will be bereft of bodily pleasures. If the 12th house is devoid of the conjunction or aspect of a benefic planet, he will fruitlessly spend his wealth and be given to much anger.* (BPHS 26:12)

- *If the 12th lord is situated in the Ascendant, the native will be a spendthrift, be weak in constitution, will suffer from phlegmatic disorders, and be devoid of wealth and learning.* (BPHS 26:133)

This is a *Dainya Parivartana Yoga* wherein the lords are in a mutual 2/12 relationship. Since this exchange involves a *trik* lord, we get the sense of a life touched by themes of sexuality, spirituality, foreign exposure and loss, thus walking a fine line between self-sacrifice and self-undoing.

Indeed, the native is something of a lost soul in search of an identity: seemingly devoid of rational intelligence or foresight, lost in dreams or fantasies, subject to errant desires. Shunned by others, and perhaps even an object of self-hatred, he can become his own worst enemy.

A pleasure seeker, his health suffers through exhaustion, eg, sexual indulgence, lack of sleep, and jet-lag. He spends money on pleasurable indulgences, which may prove to be his undoing. Although he attempts to conceal his loose morals in his sexual life, he is ultimately revealed, to his potential shame. He travels to foreign countries in pursuit of happiness, but may leave empty-handed to wander aimlessly. He seeks *moksha* in all the wrong places, and can be left with a feeling of emptiness, losing himself in the process.

He cares little about money, isn't greedy or avaricious, and spends freely or gives to charities. He is drawn unconsciously to involvement with ashrams, hospitals, or prisons. Hindsight (left eye association) is strong, so he is naturally introspective and contemplative.

Famous people with this yoga

Chuck Berry, musician; Richard Boone, actor; Tycho Brahe, astronomer; Stephen Crane, writer; Xavier Cugat, musician; Divine, transvestite/actress; King Edward VII, British royalty; Zelda Fitzgerald, flapper; Michel Foucault, philosopher; Alberto Fujimori, politician; Giuseppe Garibaldi, militarist; Garrison Keillor, broadcaster/author; Rich Little, impersonator; Madonna, singer; Mark McGwire, baseball player; Jean-Luc Ponty, musician; John Sayles, film-maker; Angel Thompson, astrologer; Jon Voight, actor; Jack Welch, corporate executive.

Case study

Madonna (Ciccone), popstar extraordinaire, has made a name for herself largely through the clever exhibitionism of her sexuality, whether through provocative stage costumes or nude photos of herself in books and magazines. Ironically, while succeeding brilliantly in the music industry, she has thus far failed miserably in movies. Religious and spiritual issues intermixed with sexuality have been constant themes in her life. Her devoutly-Catholic family was shattered when her mother died of cancer when Madonna was only six.

After a number of years during which she was agoraphobic and fearful of her own mortality, she burst out of her shell in high school to excel in the perennially popular curriculum of sex and drugs and rock'n'roll. Two marriages and one child later, she continues to show a marked interest in spiritual matters, studying Kabbalah and cultivating the persona of a spiritual seeker. To avoid the fans and paparazzi, Madonna has her homes hermetically sealed with guards, hidden cameras and an electric-eye gate, thus living in a hybrid ashram/prison.

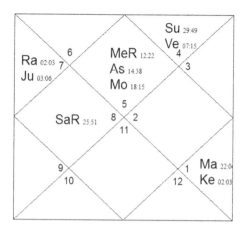

The Moon in 1st house Leo exchanges with the Sun in 12th house Cancer. Both planets are *sattvik*, which reinforces the spirituality themes of the 12th house exchange. However, the Moon is quite dark (barely more than a *tithi* past the new moon) and the Sun is *gandanta* (on the cusp of both a sign and a nakshatra), while both luminaries are aspected by strong malefics, a retrograde Saturn and a *swa* Mars. Overall, the effect is to invoke more of the "negative" 12th house aspects, ie, sexuality, physical and psychological loss, and various forms of exile, including residency abroad.

On the more positive side, the Moon in the *lagna* associates with a *dig bala* Mercury, giving her street smarts, media savvy and business acumen, since both planets are members of the *vaishya* caste, or merchant class. For its part, the Sun's association with Venus in the 12th generates a *Dharma Karma Adhipati Yoga* of 1st and 10th house lords, supporting the notion of a career that utilizes sexuality or spirituality.

Because the Sun is *gandanta* and the Moon is dark, neither is fit to assume the role of control planet. In this yoga, their coequal exchange epitomizes the themes of Self-realization versus surrender.

EXCHANGES INVOLVING THE 2ND HOUSE LORD

Exchange of 2nd and 3rd lords

Parashara says:

- *If the 2nd lord is situated in the 3rd house, the native will be a man of valor, be wise, virtuous, lustful and miserly. He will have these effects when the 2nd lord is related to a benefic; if related to a malefic, the native will be heterodox.* (BPHS 26:15)

- *If the 3rd lord happens to fall in the 2nd house, the native will be corpulent, devoid of valor, less disposed to take initiative, unhappy, and will have eyes on others' wives and others' wealth.* (BPHS 26:26)

This is a *Khala Parivartana Yoga* wherein the lords are in a mutual 2/12 relationship. Since it involves the lord of the 3rd, which is both a mild *dusthana* and an *upachaya* house, we expect a fluctuating state of difficulty, with some gradual improvement, in family and money matters.

The native lacks courage or experiences frustration of his artistic ambitions, and becomes very materialistic instead. He makes money through the application of special skills or knowledge, and achieves some status in government or industry. He may use his expertise or information to unfair advantage, eg, through insider trading, selling tainted goods, etc.

Family life is somewhat troubled, and his relationship with siblings suffers ups and downs, including estrangement and betrayal. Siblings may be very money-oriented, and yet have difficulties with their finances. Younger siblings suffer losses or changes to their circumstances.

He lacks principles in matters pertaining to wealth, family, knowledge, and sexual relations. For example, he doesn't deal fairly with family members in general. He is unscrupulous in financial transactions, and profits unfairly from other people.

Satisfying personal desires is more important than adhering to spiritual principles. For example, he might ignore marriage vows in order to satisfy a desire for a sexual relationship with someone else. A tendency to bend the law becomes especially prevalent when he experiences frustration of his desires and then in desperation seeks to break out of his impasse.

Famous people with this yoga

Lauren Bacall, actress; Russell Banks, writer; Shirley Conran, writer; Phyllis Diller, comedienne; Errol Flynn, actor; Germaine Greer, writer; Peter Jennings, news anchor; Charles Lindbergh, aviator; Baba Muktananda, spiritual leader; Tim Robbins, actor; Albert Schweitzer, humanitarian; Suzanne Somers, actress; Alexis de Tocqueville, political scientist; Sarah Vaughn, jazz singer; Oscar Wilde, writer; Steve Winwood, musician; Billy Mitchell, militarist.

Case study

Errol Flynn, the swashbuckling actor of adventure films, had a flamboyant private life indulging his lifelong passions for drinking, fighting and sex on boats. A rambunctious child with an impressive vocabulary, the "Tasmanian Devil" was thrown out of every school he attended. His father was a renowned zoologist who brought the first platypus to England, and Flynn grew up with a great love of the sea, spending his time between movies sailing around the world. Quoted as saying he liked his whiskey old and his women young, his love life was notorious – married three times, twice charged with rape, and source of the sexual catch-phrase "In like Flynn".

A legendary drinker, he eventually worked his way up to narcotics. Aside from acting, via which he burst into public view like a meteor and then burned out as quickly seven years later, his other passion was writing. He'd been a young correspondent for an Australian newspaper, and later published two novels and an autobiography. Despite his virile image, he was disqualified from WW2 military service because of a weak heart, from which he died at age 50 in the arms of his 17-year-old girlfriend.

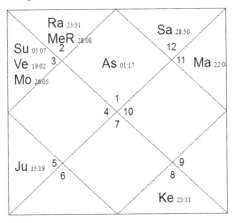

Mercury in 2nd house Taurus exchanges with Venus in 3rd house Gemini. The two are mutual friends, and in addition, both *rajasik* grahas. Right away, we get a sense of desire and activity, stimulated and supported by partners-in-crime, so to speak. Retrograde Mercury is strong but heavily afflicted by Mars, Saturn and the Rahu-Ketu axis. Venus as lord of both the 2nd and the 7th is a full *maraka* and, although free of combustion, is associated with a dark Moon in Gemini, symptomatic perhaps of Flynn's weakness for women in general and girls in particular.

On the more positive side, Venus associates with the Sun to create two other yogas – a *Dharma Karma Adhipati Yoga* via their lordships of the 5th and 7th, and a *Dhana Yoga* via the 2nd and 5th. With both luminaries and Venus in the 3rd house – a *kamasthana* (houses 3, 7 and 11 are inclined toward fulfillment of desires) – we see his fondness for the literary arts, as well as the promise and pitfalls of a life filled with adventures of all kinds.

Although Mercury is retrograde, it is heavily afflicted. Meanwhile, Venus is ordinary, associated with both luminaries, and forms multiple yogas. Thus, Venus becomes the control planet in this exchange. Its placement in the 3rd house made the pursuit of pleasure a life theme.

Exchange of 2nd and 4th lords

Parashara says:

- *In case the 2nd lord occupies the 4th house, the native is endowed with all kinds of wealth. If he is in conjunction with Jupiter or in his exaltation sign, the native will be equal to a king.* (BPHS 26:16)

- *Should the 4th lord occupy the 2nd house, the native will enjoy pleasures, be blessed with all kinds of wealth, family life and honor, and be adventurous. He will be cunning and deceptive in disposition.* (BPHS 26:38)

This is a *Maha Parivartana Yoga* wherein the lords are in a mutual 3/11 relationship. With this configuration, we expect a certain flow or facilitation of matters related to family, money, property, vehicles and education.

The native is devoted to acquiring knowledge, will receive one or more degrees, and may be involved in the fields of education or psychology. Academically-inclined, he is a visual learner, and learns best by seeing things.

He is close to his mother and enjoys financial benefits through her. She in turn enjoys gains through her own efforts or good fortune. His happiness is strongly linked to family, whether immediate or extended. In lieu of strong family attachments, he belongs to a community, or *sangha*, for the emotional or psychological comfort such a group provides.

His family is a source of wealth, particularly through property. He acquires properties and vehicles, and may be involved in businesses related to the same. He is attracted to occupations in real estate, farming, mining, house construction, hotel management, car manufacturing or sales. He may invest in luxury items such as antique furniture, cars, paintings, etc.

Famous people with this yoga

Anthony Armstrong-Jones, British royalty in-law; Alexander Graham Bell, inventor; Johannes Brahms, composer; Merle Haggard, musician; Anthony Hopkins, actor; Robbie Krieger, musician; Mary McFadden, designer; Julia Roberts, actress; George C. Scott, actor; Simone Simon, actress; Barbra Streisand, entertainer; Louis Vuitton, designer; Colleen McCullough, writer; Evelyn Waugh, writer.

Case study

Alexander Graham Bell, inventor of the telephone, was born into a family fascinated with communication. His grandfather was an eminent elocutionist, and his father was a speech pathologist who developed the first international phonetic alphabet. His mother, learning piano despite her deafness, inspired Bell's life-long desire to help the deaf and the mute. As a teenager, he constructed a "speaking machine" with a mouth, an articulated tongue and bellow lungs that could make human sounds. By age 16 he was teaching music and elocution at a boys' school, and furthering his father's work in "visible speech" techniques. This eventually brought him to the Boston School for Deaf Mutes, where he met first his future wife and later his famous protégée Helen Keller.

Although his profound scientific curiosity resulted in his inventing the telephone, for which he became rich and famous, he also developed technologies anticipating fiber-optics communications, tape and CD recordings, and the iron lung. In his later years, he developed vehicle prototypes, including giant tetrahedral kites, an airplane, and a hydrofoil that set a world speed record that stood for 44 years.

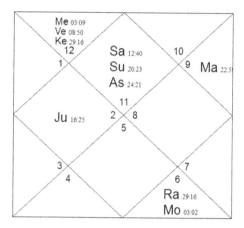

Venus in 2nd house Pisces exchanges with Jupiter in 4th house Taurus. Both are benefics. Venus commences with exaltation and, after exchange, becomes *swa* and gains *dig bala*. Jupiter goes from ordinary status to *swa*. Although Mercury and Ketu occupy the 2nd house, neither of the exchange planets are close enough in degree to become tainted by either the 8th lord or the Rahu-Ketu axis.

Pre-exchange, Venus and Mercury in the 2nd house form a *Dharma Karma Adhipati Yoga* (as lords of 4th and 5th) as well as a *Raja Yoga* (as lords of 5th and 9th). Although it can't create *Lakshmi Yoga* all on its own, exalted Venus as lord of the 9th, and *karaka* of wealth and vehicles, does sit in a money house. Thus, the 2nd house themes of speech, hearing, and wealth, as well as 4th house vehicles, were all activated by the presence of this strong *Parivartana Yoga*.

While Jupiter is ordinary, Venus is exalted, thus making it the control planet for this exchange. Its placement in the 2nd house evokes the theme of speech, to which cause much of Bell's inventive genius was applied.

Exchange of 2nd and 5th lords

Parashara says:

- *If the 2nd lord is situated in the 5th house, the native will be wealthy. His son will also be intent on earning wealth.* (BPHS 26:17)

- *If the 5th lord occupies the 2nd house, the native will have the blessing of having many sons and wealth. He will be supporter of his family, honorable, be attached to his wife, and be famous in the world.* (BPHS 26:50)

This is a *Maha Parivartana Yoga* (also a *Dhana Yoga*) wherein the lords are in a mutual 4/10 relationship. The native is naturally disposed towards intellectual pursuits, and is both an avid student and a capable teacher.

He has literary skills, a good vocabulary, and a good speaking or singing voice. Therefore, he could make a good orator, writer or politician. Furthermore, a willingness to lend dramatic effect to whatever he does could make this person a popular entertainer.

He may also be spiritually inclined, with an interest in studying and meditating upon sacred works, and the ability to memorize and recite long passages of scriptures. He could also be involved in learning or teaching mantra and meditation techniques.

The native comes from a large family, to which he is attached. The family is fortunate in money matters, values education, and is intellectually inclined. The native is thoughtful about money, and generally shrewd in investments. The native's children are dedicated students, earn handsome salaries, and establish themselves with good professions and reputations.

Famous people with this yoga

Marshall Appelwhite, cult leader; André Breton, surrealist; Catherine the Great, empress; Wes Craven, director; A.J. Cronin, writer; Indira Gandhi, politician; Harper Lee, writer; Bernard Montgomery, militarist; Robert Ripley, illustrator; Willy Shoemaker, jockey; Bruce Willis, actor; Christian Wirth, Nazi.

Case study

Catherine the Great, who was born a German princess but married into Russian royalty, transformed her nation from a backwater country into a European power. Beautiful, intelligent and ambitious, she quickly learned Russian, joined the Orthodox Church and educated herself via extensive reading. Her husband Peter III was an ugly man and incompetent ruler, eventually deposed and executed by Catherine's political allies. Although she earned a reputation for promiscuity via multiple love affairs with her officers and heads of state, her real achievement was reform. She read everything from Plato to Voltaire, and corresponded with many leading European intellectuals of the day.

Once in power, she transformed her adopted country in every way possible – introducing new agricultural techniques in farming regions, building roads and bridges, creating schools of medicine and mining, facilitating factory start-ups, importing British science and technology, abolishing export duties, conducting mapping and census, building hospitals and schools, amassing art collections and promoting Russian culture. The only ambition she failed to realize in her 34-year reign was the abolition of serfdom, a political move that might have destabilized the country that she'd worked so hard to change.

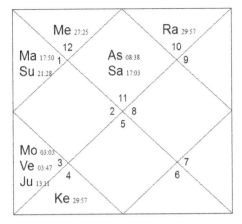

Jupiter in 5th house Gemini exchanges with debilitated Mercury in 2nd house Pisces. These two *jiva tattva* planets are strongly associated with matters of the intellect. In addition to its debilitation, Mercury is also hemmed by three powerful malefics – *swa* Saturn on one side, and *swa* Mars and *uchcha* Sun on the other. Jupiter, on the other hand, is associated with the Moon to form a *Kesari Yoga*, and with Venus to form a pair of *Dhana Yogas*. In fact, the exchange of 2nd lord Jupiter with 5th lord Mercury is itself a *Dhana Yoga*. Jupiter's position in the 5th also qualifies it as the foundation of a *Kalanidhi Yoga*, because it is in the sign of Mercury and in association with Venus.

Cultured (2nd), intelligent, studious (2nd) and charming, Catherine was also ambitious, cruel, egotistical and domineering. A passionate woman, she had a series of at least 22 young lovers. By age 67, she had lost all her teeth (2nd) and was plagued by debilitating varicose veins.

Since Mercury is debilitated while Jupiter is merely ordinary, it has the relative strength to function as control planet for this exchange. Jupiter's placement in the 5th house remains the signature of Catherine's intelligence and her intellectual reformation of Russia.

Exchange of 2nd and 6th lords

Parashara says:

- *Should the 2nd lord occupy the 6th house and be in conjunction with a benefic, the native will gain wealth through his enemies; if with a malefic, the native will have loss through his enemies and be weak-thighed.* (BPHS 26:18)

- *In case the 6th lord has fallen in the 2nd house, the native will be adventurous, illustrious in his family, and he will live in alien countries or foreign lands, be happy, be a good speaker, and be always interested in his own work.* (BPHS 26:62)

This is a *Dainya Parivartana Yoga* wherein the lords are in a mutual 5/9 relationship from *artha* houses. Although the 6th is a *trikasthana*, it is also an *upachaya* house, wherein the situation is amenable to improvement over time.

The native experiences money problems of one kind or another through poor saving habits, theft, unpaid loans, damaged goods, lawsuits, lost items, and/or expensive health care. Health concerns include bad teeth, bad breath, poor vision, allergies, food poisoning, bad diet, substance abuse and thyroid problems.

Similarly, the native may have problems with learning, retaining or expressing ideas, eg, poor study habits or memory, lack of imagination, foul language, speech impediment, poor vocabulary, or lack of oratorical skills.

The native's spouse will have poor health. (The 7th is the spouse, so if we rotate the chart to adopt its perspective, the 2nd is the 8th from the spouse, and the 6th is the 12th from the spouse; therefore, both are *trik* lords from the perspective of the spouse.) Maternal uncles may undertake long journeys.

He gains employment through the service trades, especially those related to health, animals, the workplace, and the environment. Someone in the family may also be employed in health care, particularly veterinary science.

Famous people with this yoga

Kareem Abdul-Jabbar, basketball star; Prince Albert, British royalty; Carol Burnett, comedienne; Ram Dass, spiritual author; Situ Rimpoche, spiritual leader; Dean Stockwell, actor; Gene Tunney, boxer; Mike Wallace, TV personality.

Case study

Ram Dass, born as Richard Alpert, studied psychology with a specialization in human motivation and personality development. He served on the faculties at Stanford, the University of California, and Harvard University. While at Harvard, his explorations of human consciousness led him to collaborate with Timothy Leary, Aldous Huxley and Allen Ginsberg, in using LSD. Because of this controversial research, he was subsequently fired from Harvard.

After a trip to India during which he met his guru, he was renamed Ram Dass, "Servant of God", and changed his life direction to pursue a wide range of spiritual practices, becoming involved in many humanitarian projects, including agricultural reform and treatment of blindness in third world countries. He has written several books, the most notable of which was the bestseller *Be Here Now*, a classic spiritual guide. In 1997, he suffered a left-brain hemorrhage that paralyzed much of the right side of his body, but he continues to make public appearances.

~

Debilitated Mars in 2nd house Cancer exchanges with debilitated Moon in 6th house Scorpio. Although the exchange between these two house lords gives an impetus towards the pursuit of *artha*, or security, as a life goal, it was not his own security but that of the disenfranchised that seemed to motivate his humanitarian actions.

Indeed, since both planets are in water signs, we could further rationalize that the spiritual resolution of this double-debilitation required some form of *bhakti* yoga.

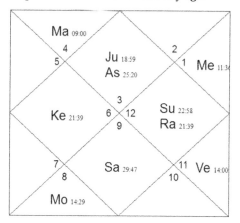

Although he gained fame and notoriety for his use, or substance abuse (2nd house) of psychedelics, Ram Dass did go on to author at least three books on spirituality. Interestingly enough for someone with a 6th house exchange, his adopted name Ram Dass means "servant to Lord Ram." He has also worked as an activist for Seva Foundation, whose causes include environmental (6th house) issues, and fighting blindness (2nd house) in third world countries.

With neither planet assuming clear control over the exchange, the themes of authorship and service remain coequals as per the 2nd/6th-house associations of this yoga.

Exchange of 2nd and 7th lords

Parashara says:

- *In the event of the 2nd lord falling in the 7th house, the native will be apt to traverse another's wife and be a physician. If the 2nd lord in the 7th house is in conjunction with or is aspected by a malefic, his wife will be a harlot.* (BPHS 26:19)

- *If the 7th lord is placed in the 2nd house, the native will have many wives, will gain wealth through his wife and will be of procrastinating nature.* (BPHS 26:74)

This is a *Maha Parivartana Yoga* wherein the lords are in a mutual 6/8 relationship from *maraka* houses. For this combination, we generally expect mixed reviews within a marital context, especially wherein the partners do not see "eye-to-eye" or one of then "has eyes for another".

The native gains through marriage, and enjoys a good family life, but has difficulty maintaining a monogamous relationship. He experiences strong attractions to members of the opposite sex, such that personal relationships tend to be sexually-motivated. Relationship with in-laws may thus be adversely affected.

His spouse is a dominant personality and may be equally suspect in terms of needing to explore relationships outside the marriage. His spouse suffers mentally, emotionally or physically, possibly as a consequence of a turbulent marital life, and may experience premature illness or death.

Business and financial relationships are carried out at a distance, via the agency of foreign partners, or in the form of travel to foreign countries. Whatever money he earns is shared with his partner.

Second marriages would be favored during the conjoined periods of the two house lords in exchange.

Famous people with this yoga

Dino de Laurentis, producer; Hans Eysenck, psychologist & astrologer; Gennifer Flowers, political mistress; Daryl Hannah, actress; Jean Harlow, actress; Andy Kaufman, actor; Jack Kerouac, writer; Oliver North, patriot; Walter Schirra, astronaut; Alicia Silverstone, actress.

Case study

Jack Kerouac, a "solitary crazy Catholic mystic", was a founding member of the "Beat Generation", a term he coined. His older brother died at age nine, and his father died an alcoholic. Although Kerouac won a football scholarship to Columbia, he dropped out and hit the road, crisscrossing the continent several times, writing about his experiences and picking up bad habits along the way, mainly heavy drinking and Benzedrine use. He wrote his famous novel, *On the Road*, in three coffee-fueled weeks, and another novel, *The Subterraneans*, in a Benzedrine-powered rush of just three days. Along with fellow beatniks Allen Ginsberg and William Burroughs, he forged new literary territory.

Success came late, and he had trouble dealing with both his new-found fame and the critics who disliked a prose style that violated so many rules of syntax and grammar. Although repeatedly drawn into relationships, none lasted long, and his two marriages ended in divorce. In later years, he became a recluse, living with his mother and playing solitary card games he'd invented to simulate baseball and football games. He died of cirrhosis of the liver at age 47, leaving an estate of less than $100.

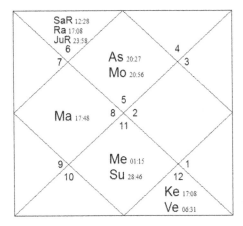

Saturn in 2nd house Virgo exchanges with Mercury in 7th house Aquarius, both *maraka* houses. Saturn forms a *Dharma Karma Adhipati Yoga* with Jupiter in the 2nd, although it is afflicted by the Rahu-Ketu axis. Mercury is associated with the Sun, forming a *Budhaditya Yoga* and two *Dhana Yogas*.

Post-exchange, Saturn joins the Sun in the 7th to form a lusty combination, while Mercury moves to Virgo where it forms a complex with the equally mutable Piscean Venus at the opposite end of the Rahu-Ketu axis. Both Mercury and Saturn are considered to be neuter or sex-less planets (Mercury too "young" and Saturn too "old"), which may reflect on Kerouac's sexual ambivalence. Themes of the 2nd and 7th houses played out in authorship, substance abuse, troubled family life, wandering travel and dysfunctional relationships.

Best known for his book, *The Dharma Bums*, Kerouac was prolific and authored 21 books in all. With the axis of planets through his 2nd/8th houses, he suffered from both alcoholism and methedrine abuse. He was discharged from the merchant marine for psychiatric reasons, and was briefly jailed in connection with a murder. Bisexual, he married three times, carried a torch for fellow Beatnik Neal Cassady, and meticulously kept an archive of every sexual experience he had with a woman.

While Mercury is ordinary, Saturn is retrograde, thus making it the control planet for this exchange. Its mixed association with Rahu and a bright Jupiter in the 2nd house lent fuel to both his prolific writing and substance abuse.

Exchange of 2nd and 8th lords

Parashara says:

- *Should the 2nd lord happen to be placed in the 8th house, the native is endowed with abundant land wealth, but he will have little marital felicity and be bereft of happiness through elder brother.* (BPHS 26:20)

- *If the 8th lord is placed in the 2nd house, the native will be devoid of physical vigor, will possess little wealth, and will not regain lost wealth.* (BPHS 26:86)

This is a *Dainya Parivartana Yoga* wherein the lords are in a mutual 7/7 relationship. This *sambandha* of mutual aspect also serves to strengthen (and aggravate) the significations of the exchange.

Because the respective lords of one's own money versus another's money are being exchanged, the notion of currency or financial exchange is one interpretation. This could manifest in a constructive manner, eg, via a banker or investment broker who manages other people's money or, less constructively, as a thief or swindler.

In a similar vein, we could also interpret the exchange in light of education or knowledge. Acquired knowledge may be specialized, and transmitted via an oral tradition in such areas as mysticism, the occult, or the alternative healing arts. For example, this could appear in the chart of a scholar of antiquities, a linguist, an occultist, or a practitioner of *Jyotisha*, *ayurveda*, *shiatsu* or Traditional Chinese Medicine.

The native may have unexpected reversals, ie, things going from good to bad, or vice versa, in matters affecting both the oral cavity and the vision. For example, linguistic skills versus speech impediments, oratorical abilities versus foul language, balanced diet versus substance abuse, clear versus blurry vision.

Financial affairs may also go through ups and downs – there could be inheritances and gains from insurance, but also gambling, irrecoverable business losses, demands for alimony, and chronic indebtedness.

By the same token, family life may exhibit a cycle of peaks and troughs, including financial crises that affect the family fortunes, or highly-charged emotional situations that challenge family values.

Famous people with this yoga

Charles Addams, cartoonist; Sam Cooke, performer; Billy Corgan, musician; Sir Arthur Conan Doyle, writer; Robert Duvall, actor; Peter Gabriel, musician; Franz Joseph Haydn, composer; Manik Chand Jain, astrologer; Jimmy Page, musician; George Lincoln Rockwell, American Nazi; Linda Ronstadt, singer; Cheryl Tiegs, model.

Case study

Jimmy Page, one of the greatest rock guitarists of all time, originally wanted to be a biological researcher but left school at age 16 to pursue music. In 1968 he founded Led Zeppelin, which became one of the biggest rock bands in the world, while developing a reputation for excess and debauchery: trashed hotel rooms, kinky sex and heavy use of drugs and alcohol. For several years, Page was a regular heroin user.

Fascinated with the occult, Page owned an occult bookstore and purchased the former rural retreat of Aleister Crowley (notorious occultist and designer of the Thoth tarot deck) as one of his homes. His arcane interests were reflected via astrological symbols in the band's album covers and stage costumes. One biographer speculated Page had made a pact with the Devil to ensure Led Zep's success, and one interpretation of "Stairway to Heaven" claimed it contained satanic reverse-audio messages. An avid collector, Page owns roughly 1500 guitars.

In recent years he's been involved in various charity concerts and charity work, particularly the Action for Brazil's Children Trust, for which he was awarded the Order of the British Empire in 2005.

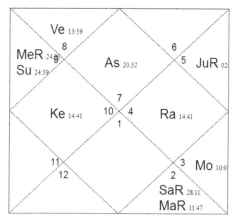

Venus in 2nd house Scorpio exchanges with Mars in 8th house Taurus. Mars retrograde is strong and joins forces with an equally strong retrograde Saturn in the 8th to form both a *Dharma Karma Adhipati Yoga* and a *Dhana Yoga*. Because *lagnesh* Venus is in mutual aspect with both Mars and Saturn, it further generates another four yogas – a *Dharma Karma Adhipati Yoga* and a *Dhana Yoga* with Mars, and two *Dharma Karma Adhipati Yogas* with Saturn.

The negative effect of two powerful malefics on this yoga skewed Page into dark territory – his heroin addiction, his fascination with the occult, and some unsubstantiated rumors about sex with juvenile girls. On the plus side, however, he was well-educated and soft-spoken, and created a massive transfer of wealth from pop fans into the bank accounts of Led Zeppelin. Equally positive, he turned his own significant wealth back into several charities.

Interestingly enough, Page is one of the relatively few people (3% of the population) who have two *Parivartana Yogas*, the second being an exchange between the 3rd and 11th lords. Although discussed in greater detail in the relevant section, this yoga is indicative of financial or social (11th house) success through the arts or sports (3rd house), a feat that Page achieved via his mastery of the guitar.

While Venus is ordinary, Mars is retrograde, thus making it the control planet for this exchange. Its placement in the 8th house simply recalls Page's fascination with the occult in his younger years, followed by his charity work in his mature years.

Exchange of 2nd and 9th lords

Parashara says:

- *Should the 2nd lord be placed in the 9th house, the native will be wealthy, diligent and skillful. He remains sickly in childhood but happy in the remaining years of life. He visits shrines and observes religious rites, etc.* (BPHS 26:21)

- *Should the 9th lord be situated in the 2nd house, the native will be learned, popular, wealthy, lustful, and be blessed with happiness through sons and wife.* (BPHS 26:98)

This is a *Maha Parivartana Yoga* (also a *Dhana Yoga*) wherein the lords are in a mutual 6/8 relationship. The native is born with a silver spoon in his mouth, or may be considered "silver-tongued". His family is blessed with good education and wealth. He receives money from foreign sources and conveyances.

His father is affiliated with universities, courts of law or the government. Because the exchanging lords are in a 6/8 relationship, his father may be afflicted with some common ailment or disease, or may experience a fluctuating state of employment.

The native tends to speak the truth, or dispenses wisdom, such as would a professor, author, orator or counselor. (*Vak shuddhi, vak siddhi.*) He often manifests other good qualities associated with the mouth, eg, eloquent speech, good vocabulary, fine teeth, good singing voice, and/or good diet.

He travels in pursuit of his education, favoring subjects such as finance, mathematics, languages and education. He receives formal instruction from a teacher or guru who is a good orator and an expert in the *shastras* or comparable classical works.

Famous people with this yoga

Giulio Andreotti, politician; Drew Barrymore, actress; John Belushi, comedian; Celine Dion, singer; Hans Holzer, occult writer; Edna St-Vincent Millay, poet; Princess Nour Pahlavi, Iranian royalty; William Penn, colonist; Rafael Sabatini, novelist; Gilles Villeneuve, race-car driver; Kanye West, musician.

Case study

Celine Dion, popstar diva, was born into a highly musical family, the youngest of 14 children, with a strong attachment to her father. She began performing in her parents' piano bar at five years old. By age 17 she'd emerged as an international talent. Her manager, who later became her husband, mortgaged his house to produce her first album. Over the years, she racked up one industry award after another and broke records for albums sold, winning Oscars for both *Beauty and the Beast* and *Titanic* soundtracks, the latter album becoming the top-selling soundtrack album of all time. In total, Dion has sold over 200 million albums worldwide. In addition, she performed under contract at Caesar's Palace in Las Vegas for a five-year stint reputedly worth over $200 million.

A supporter of charities, financially generous with her original family, and devoted to her spouse and children, she remains a shining inspiration to every singer with a dream. Along the way, there have been a few legal complications, notably a lawsuit against the *National Enquirer*, and another involving her husband's alleged sexual harassment of a Vegas employee, both suits successfully dismissed.

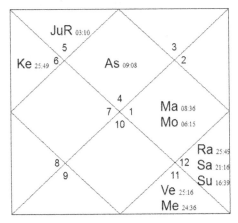

Jupiter in 2nd house Leo exchanges with Sun in 9th house Pisces. The exchange also forms a *Dhana Yoga*. Retrograde Jupiter is powerful, aspected only by benefics Mercury and Venus to form a *Sushubha Yoga*. This plays out in several 2nd house themes – her huge family of 13 siblings, her great vocal talent with its five-octave range, and her subsequent wealth as a pop diva.

The exchange with the 9th house invokes foreign income (a hit in France when she was only 14), a formative relationship with a musical father (*karaka* Sun), and a father-figure in a husband (Sun with 7th lord Saturn) 26 years her senior. Although three malefics in the 9th house threaten court cases, the exchange has also helped to resolve them. She successfully sued *The National Enquirer* $20 million for falsely stating she was pregnant with twins.

With the benefic exchange of 2nd and 9th lords, she's also been generous with her family, buying houses for her parents, giving her siblings large sums of money, and employing many among them. The exchange supports 2nd house matters: her diet (she neither smokes nor drinks) and languages (having zealously studied Berlitz English to prepare for the American pop market). She also owns a chain of restaurants in Quebec, and has her own lines of eye-wear and perfume, all 2nd house significations.

While the Sun is ordinary, Jupiter is retrograde, thus making it the control planet for this exchange. Its placement in the 2nd house sums up the major themes of Dion's life – family, voice and the great wealth that sprang from her singing.

Exchange of 2nd and 10th lords

Parashara says:

- *In case the 2nd lord is situated in the 10th house, the native will be libidinous, honorable and learned, will have many wives but will be bereft of filial happiness.* (BPHS 26:22)

- *If the 10th lord occupies the 2nd house, the native will be wealthy, virtuous, honored by the King (or the Government), charitable and endowed with paternal and other bliss.* (BPHS 26:110)

This is a *Maha Parivartana Yoga* wherein the lords are in a mutual 5/9 relationship from *artha* houses. The native's family is wealthy, and has a reputation built on financial or business success. If one of the planets involved is slow-moving, eg, Jupiter or Saturn, it could be old money, but if they are fast, eg, the Moon or Mercury, it's more likely to be new money.

The native gets a practical education that has currency in society. He maintains his family wealth, and grows his own capital by earning a good income from profession or business.

If the planets in exchange are benefics, the earnings are through honest means; if malefics, then underhanded.

He achieves considerable status in his community, and has a voice in their assembly. He has a face that is recognizable and/or attractive to the public. He has the opportunity to speak in public, or things that he says privately become public. If the planets in exchange are benefics, he uses his authority wisely; if malefics, he is corrupt and abuses his authority. Similarly, an exchange of benefics suggests spoken truth and wisdom, while malefics mean cheap talk and lies.

This combination favors careers in finance, precious metals, restaurants, public speaking, dentistry, cosmetics, nutrition, currency exchange, speech therapy education, or writing.

Famous people with this yoga

Sri Meher Baba, spiritual leader; Rick Danko, musician; Benny Hill, comedian; Willie Nelson, singer; Nityananda, holy man; Bangalore Rao, astrologer; Brad Steiger, occult writer; Julius Streicher, Nazi publisher; Maurice Utrillo, artist; Jules Verne, writer; Swami Vivekananda, spiritual leader.

Case study

Sri Meher Baba, dubbed "The Awakener", the Avatar of Kali Yuga, was initiated at age 20 into god-realization by the female saint Hazrat Babajan. After a period of intense spiritual activity, he undertook a vow of silence that lasted almost 30 years. Despite his silence, he served the needs of humanity on a material as well as a spiritual level by establishing schools and hospitals, personally caring for lepers, the mad and religious ecstatics. Through the medium of gestures and an alphabet board, he dictated several books and spiritual messages to his followers.

He traveled widely in India and Pakistan, and made 13 trips to the West, during which he made many notable converts among cultural icons of the day, including Pete Townshend of the Who, and other artists. Throughout the 60s, he spoke widely about the dangers of drugs on a physical, psychological and spiritual level. Although concerned about the materialism of the age, one of his main teachings was that the material and spiritual must go hand in hand, that one cannot stay in a spiritual retreat one's whole life, but that God must be found in the world, through service and selfless action.

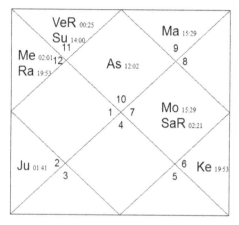

Venus in 2nd house Aquarius exchanges with Saturn in 10th house Libra. The two are mutual friends, both retrograde and therefore powerful. For this ascendant, exalted Saturn is also *lagnesh*, and its friend Venus is *yogakaraka* (ruling both *trikona* and *kendra*). Venus is with one luminary, the Sun, but far enough away to escape combustion. Saturn, along with the other luminary the Moon, forms a *Dharma Karma Adhipati Yoga* in the 10th. Post-exchange, Saturn resides in the 2nd house (speech) with its enemy, the Sun, but because of its degree position, no matter whether Saturn assumes the exact place of Venus or carries its own degree into the 2nd, Saturn does not become combust after exchange.

The 2nd house governs what goes in and out of the mouth. As such, it rules food and drink, but also voice and its fluency, by which we mean both physical and mental qualities. Fluent in several languages, Baba spoke out against drugs. He was also a poet and multi-instrumentalist with an excellent singing voice.

The 10th house is a *karmasthana*, and its exchange with the 2nd encouraged Baba's fasting and silence. In the process, he began his practice of demanding strict discipline and obedience from his disciples. *Do as I say, and do as I do.*

Venus and Saturn are both retrograde, but Saturn is also exalted, thus making it the control planet for this exchange. Its status in the 10th represents his enduring reputation as a guru of asceticism and silence.

Exchange of 2nd and 11th lords

Parashara says:

- *Should the 2nd lord be in the 11th house, the native will enjoy all kinds of wealth and gains, will be ever diligent, honorable and famous.* (BPHS 26:23)

- *Should the 11th lord be placed in the 2nd house, the native will be endowed with all kinds of wealth and all kinds of accomplishments, be charitable, religious and always happy.* (BPHS 26:122)

This is a *Maha Parivartana Yoga* wherein the lords are in a mutual 4/10 relationship from wealth (*dhana*) houses. With this pattern, we expect the yoga to manifest its positive results within the contexts of family, education and wealth.

The native's family, especially his elder siblings, and paternal aunts and uncles, will be wealthy and well-educated. One or the other of these is likely to be involved in a business having to do with banking or finance.

He makes good money in business, and it seems that money is always flowing in his direction. Even his money is working to make more money through dividend-paying equity investments and interest-bearing instruments such as bonds. Furthermore, his financial fortunes improve after marriage.

His friends become part of his extended family. He has an active social conscience, and lives his life accordingly. He joins community groups or social networks. He belongs to a *sangha* or is associated with some group whose common interests include investment, education, nutrition, politics, entertainment, public speaking or singing.

He may receive awards, honors or social distinctions accompanied by financial prizes.

Famous people with this yoga

Bjorn Borg, tennis player; William Jennings Bryan, politician; Carrie Fisher, actress/writer; Gustave Flaubert, writer; Joan Grant, writer; James Herbert, writer; David Janssen, actor; Curt Jurgens, actor; Caroline Kennedy, American "royalty"; Patricia Krenwinkle, cult killer; Maurice Maeterlinck, philosopher; Ross Macdonald, writer; Wayne Newton, entertainer; Joe Pesci, actor; Oscar Pistorius, paralympic athlete; Pete Rose, baseball player; Frank Sinatra, entertainer; Oprah Winfrey, talk show hostess.

Case study

Oprah Winfrey, talk show host, has been dubbed the "Queen of all Media" and is, according to some, the most influential woman in the world. Ranked the richest African-American of the 20th century, America's only black billionaire was born into poverty to a single teenage mother. She experienced considerable hardship in her childhood, getting raped at age nine, becoming pregnant at 14, and losing her only son in infancy. During high school she landed a job in radio, went on at age 19 to co-anchor local news, and subsequently graduated to daytime talk shows. The rest is history.

Oprah had three half-siblings, one of whom died of cocaine abuse, another put up for a adoption, and a third dead of AIDS. Nicknamed "the Preacher" because of her ability as a child to recite Bible verses, she won an oratory contest in high school that earned her a full university scholarship. She has co-authored five books and played in more than a dozen movies. She is an active philanthropist and a major social influence, with the power to turn books into bestsellers and political endorsements into presidential candidates.

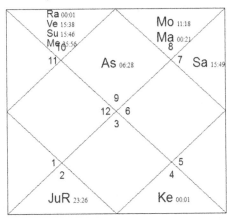

Venus in 2nd house Capricorn exchanges with Saturn in 11th house Libra. The two planets are mutual friends in money houses. The 2nd lord Saturn is dignified by sign both before and after exchange. Venus forms a *Dhana Yoga* with the Sun. Before and after exchange, both Venus and Saturn are totally combust, which has the effect of harming family and/or friends.

Aside from the obvious wealth-generating aspects of this combination, we should note the various themes of the 2nd house that have come to the fore in her life: eating and weight loss, confessions of substance abuse, family problems, oratorical skills, authorship, love of books and education.

Equally well, the 11th house themes are observed through social networking and influence, political activism, gay rights advocacy, high-profile friendships (Maria Shriver and Maya Angelou) and public honors – honorary Harvard doctorate, and a Presidential Medal of Freedom.

While Venus is totally combust, Saturn is exalted, thus making it the obvious control planet in this exchange. Its placement in the 11th house gives testimony to Oprah's income, her political influence and her status as the "Queen of all Media."

Exchange of 2nd and 12th lords

Parashara says:

- *If the 2nd lord occupies the 12th house, the combination makes the native adventurous, devoid of wealth, dependent on others, and keeps him bereft of the happiness of the eldest son.* (BPHS 26:24)

- *Should the 12th lord be situated in the 2nd house, the native will always spend money on auspicious deeds, be religious, will speak sweetly, and be blessed with virtues and happiness.* (BPHS 26:134)

This is a *Dainya Parivartana Yoga* wherein the lords are in a mutual 3/11 relationship. Expense and diet control become two major themes for this particular configuration.

The native experiences large fluctuations of income and expenses, perhaps stemming from import/export activities. He takes up foreign employment, or enjoys income from a foreign source. He doesn't concern himself very much with money, and is generous in donating to worthy causes, or careless in spending money on sex or travel (depending on whether the respective lords are aspected by benefics or malefics).

He has problems with his eyes or oral cavity, particularly if either house lord is afflicted. Mouth problems include bad teeth, foul language, untruthfulness, and poor dietary habits. The person could have crooked teeth, or even be cross-eyed.

He is separated from his family due to foreign travel, hospitalization or incarceration. A family member takes up foreign residence for a period of time, maybe even immigrates.

He is sexually attracted to a member of the extended family, eg, the mother's older sibling. His second marriage is based upon sexual attraction and the spouse is aggressive.

Drugs or alcohol are linked to sleep and sex, such that he needs assistance to fall asleep or perform sexually. Conversely, substance abuse depresses his energy level, affecting wakefulness and/or libido.

Moksha, spiritual liberation, may come with difficulty through *jnana yoga*, the yoga of knowledge, or devotion to *shastra*.

Famous people with this yoga

Bertolt Brecht, playwright; Alexandra David-Neel, mystic & writer; Queen Elizabeth II, British royalty; Squeaky Fromm, failed assassin; Spalding Gray, humorist; William Randolph Hearst, publisher; Bob Jansky, astrologer; Rodney King, LAPD victim; Gordon Lightfoot, musician; James Lovell, astronaut; Marion March, astrologer; Francois Mitterand, politician; Roger Zelazny, sci-fi writer.

Case study

Queen Elizabeth II, reigning monarch of British royalty, has had a checkered life. On the one hand, she was born into wealth, with estates and parties and horses and dogs, yet during WW2 she was an ambulance mechanic and knitted socks for the troops. She married a Prince (of Greece) and after the birth of their son, Prince Charles, followed Philip's naval career to Malta.

Elizabeth is considered one of the world's wealthiest women. But in 1992, she agreed to pay income tax on her personal income, the first time in the history of the monarchy. And as Queen, she has presided over the sunset of the British Empire – during her reign, 40 former British colonies, protectorates and territories have been granted their independence.

In her lifetime, the Royal Family has "lost ground" in multiple ways. Overall, media scrutiny of the Royal Family, especially at the death of Diana, Princess of Wales in 1997, led to an intense re-evaluation of the role of the British monarchy near the end of the century.

Never mind the loss of wealth, the "loss of face" for the Royal family could plot a soap opera. Her uncle King Edward VIII abdicated to marry a commoner, making her father King George VI and putting her in line for next Queen. Her sister Anne was an alcoholic, her other sister Margaret a divorcee. The Charles and Diana marriage was such a mess that it ended with Diana dead. Charles got his phone hacked while telling Camilla he wanted to be reincarnated as her knickers. Andrew and Fergie split, leaving Fergie sucking someone else's toes on a beach to the delight of paparazzi. Prince Harry was caught naked on video in Vegas. Then Andrew again, accused of sexual abuse and taking bribes…

No wonder Elizabeth needs a martini at tea-time.

~

Mars in 2nd house Capricorn exchanges with Saturn in 12th house Scorpio. Both are malefics who happen to be enemies, and together they form, whether before or after exchange, a *Papa Kartari Yoga* with Ketu in the ascendant.

Mars and Jupiter form a pair of *Dharma Karma Adhipati Yogas*. Both pre- and post-exchange, Saturn lends its influence to partially relieve Jupiter's debilitation.

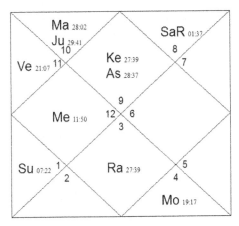

Although Saturn is retrograde, its strength is trumped by Mars in exaltation, which makes the latter the more likely choice as control planet in this exchange. Its position in the 2nd house speaks to its role in perpetuating the themes of wealth and family, indeed dynasty.

EXCHANGES INVOLVING THE 3RD HOUSE LORD

Exchange of 3rd and 4th lords

Parashara says:

- *Should the 3rd lord be situated in the 4th house, the native will be happy, wealthy and intelligent but will acquire a vicious wife.* (BPHS 26:28)

- *If the 4th lord be placed in the 3rd house, the native will be valorous, will have servants, be liberal, virtuous and charitable, and will have self-earned wealth and be free from diseases.* (BPHS 26:39)

This is a *Khala Parivartana Yoga* wherein the lords are in a mutual 2/12 relationship. The native is physically restless, happiest when in motion, and is therefore not inclined to settle down for long. He changes relationships, jobs, residence and vehicles frequently.

He is adventurous and courageous, such that he is drawn to professions that offer some element of risk, eg, the arts, sports, firefighting, police, or military occupations. His hands may play an active role in what he does for a living.

His mother's happiness, or his relationship with her, is disturbed. She experiences loss or unwelcome change in her life. She may move frequently, be frequently "off-balance", and suffer debility of a physical or psychological nature.

Although the native himself suffers breaks in his education, he is an auditory learner, and learns best by hearing things. An education in the arts or the trades is favored.

His siblings are well-educated, and enjoy financial security. Brothers and sisters are close to his mother, and become involved in real estate, farming, mining, and the transportation or hospitality industries.

Famous people with this yoga

Scott Adams, cartoonist; Burt Bacharach, composer; José Raul Capablanca, chess grandmaster; Prince Charles, British royalty; Francis Ford Coppola, film-maker; Noel Coward, playwright; Ray Davies, musician; Alain Delon, actor; Shannen Doherty, actress; Federico Fellini, director; Joseph Goebbels, Nazi; Washington Irving, writer; James Jones, writer; Alan Ladd, producer; John Malkovich, actor; Ray Manzarek, musician; Sal Mineo, actor; Martin Scorsese, director; Daryl Sittler, hockey player; Sir Arthur Sullivan, composer.

Case study

Noel Coward was a prolific British writer for the performance arts, writing over 50 plays, 100 songs, and novels and short stories. He also performed as an actor and singer in many of his productions, and later as a director and producer. Despite a spotty education, at the peak of his career he was the highest-paid playwright in the world.

Born in the suburbs, he was introduced early on to British high society and subsequently cultivated an image (dressing gown and cigarette holder) that became his signature look. Although his admitted goal was only to entertain, many of his plays were considered shocking in their day, bringing to light the shenanigans of the upper class, including infidelity, drug use, *ménage à trois*, bisexuality and homosexuality.

He was himself a closet homosexual during an era when self-disclosure was socially risky, but he was widely admired for his brilliant intellect and biting wit. Mentally as well as physically restless, he was a workaholic who declared that "work was more fun than fun." He was eventually knighted for his contribution to the arts, and received a Tony Award for lifetime achievement.

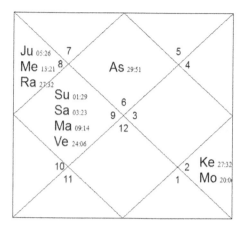

Jupiter in Scorpio 3rd exchanges with Mars in Sagittarius 4th. The two are mutual friends. Jupiter forms two *Dharma Karma Adhipati Yogas* with *lagnesh* Mercury, a *Kesari Yoga* with an exalted Moon in the 9th, and a *Guruchandala Yoga* with Rahu in the 3rd. Furthermore, the presence of Jupiter at one end of the Rahu-Ketu axis helps to stabilize a weak *Kala Sarpa* configuration, arguably making it more of a yoga than a dosha.

Mars as 8th lord is involved in multiple (mixed, not pure) *Viparita Yogas* with 6th lord Saturn and 12th lord the Sun. The addition of Venus in the 4th house constitutes a *Pravrajya Yoga*.

3rd house themes were evident in his writing and life-long devotion to the performance arts. The cluster of warring malefics in the 4th house reflected his incomplete education and handicapped mother.

He spoke with characteristic clipped diction, a form of speech he adopted to accommodate his nearly-deaf mother. In the 1950s he left England for tax reasons to live in Bermuda, Jamaica and Switzerland. Three malefics in the 4th, along with the 3rd/4th exchange contributed to tubercular complications and death by heart attack.

Since both planets are ordinary, control is not immediately obvious. Mars, however, is doubly afflicted by malefics while Jupiter, although on the nodal axis, does enjoy the aspect of an exalted and almost-full Moon. It's a judgment call, but it's safe to regard Jupiter as the control planet for this exchange. Its 3rd house placement epitomizes Coward's success as a performer and writer.

Exchange of 3rd and 5th lords

Parashara says:

- *In case the 3rd lord is placed in the 5th house, the native will be blessed with sons and be worthy. If he is in conjunction with or is aspected by a malefic planet, the native's wife is of a cruel nature.* (BPHS 26:29)

- *In case the 5th lord is situated in the 3rd house, the native will be dear to his brothers, be a tale bearer and miserly, and is always interested in his own work.* (BPHS 26:51)

This is a *Khala Parivartana Yoga* wherein the lords are in a mutual 3/11 relationship. The mixed results of this yoga flow easily into manifestation, with generally positive effects for his siblings, but somewhat negative effects for his children.

The person is mentally restless and always thinking of doing something. Because of a mental preoccupation with sex, his practical intelligence sinks to a lower plane. Due to a propensity for being easily distracted, this will also make meditation difficult. On the other hand, he enjoys games or pastimes that require mental or digital dexterity, eg, cards, chess, backgammon, crossword puzzles, or craft work.

He is courageous and prepared to take risks, intellectually and physically. This favors careers such as engineering, physics and military science, or anything requiring a technical turn of mind. He may also have talent in the arts that require manual dexterity, such as painting, drawing, music, and journalism (especially travel writing).

His siblings are interested in literature, spiritual pursuits, or sports. Benefics in exchange favor the arts, while malefics favor sports. Younger siblings are likely to take frequent short journeys.

His children are independent and earn good salaries. They are not subservient to their parents (may in fact be disobedient or rebellious), and tend to treat them more as friends.

Famous people with this yoga

Olivia Barclay, astrologer; Sarah Bernhardt, actress; Frank Borman, astronaut; Herb Elliot, track & field star; Connie Francis, singer; Gus Grissom, astronaut; Hugh Hefner, publisher; Immanuel Kant, philosopher; Nicolo Machiavelli, political theorist; Rainer Maria Rilke, poet; Nicole Brown Simpson, murder victim; Stephen Sondheim, composer; Keith Urban, musician; Tammy Wynette, singer.

Case study

Sarah Bernhardt was born the illegitimate daughter of a prostitute, but eventually became one of the most renowned actresses of her time. After being expelled from France's prestigious theatre *Comédie Française*, she resumed the life of a courtesan to which her mother had introduced her, and made considerable money during those years. When she later resumed her stage career to achieve success and fame as a serious dramatic actress, people began to call her "the Divine Sarah."

Along the way, she accumulated a series of lovers from among the best-known artists of the day, not to mention a few members of European nobility, conducting her affairs with a maximum of frenzy and tragedy worthy of her dramatic background. She was married only once for less than one year.

A versatile artist, she studied both painting and sculpture, and her works were subsequently exhibited and well received. Perhaps anticipating method acting, she acquired a coffin in which she often slept, saying it helped her understand her many tragic roles.

After injuring a knee during a performance, the leg never healed properly, gangrene set in, and the entire leg had to be amputated. Undaunted, she continued to perform onstage, and died of kidney failure at age 78.

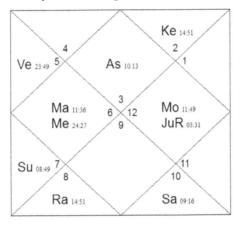

Venus in 3rd house Leo exchanges with the Sun in 5th house Libra. The two are mutual enemies, uninvolved in any other yoga. The Sun is debilitated, hemmed by malefics and tightly aspected by a powerful Saturn in the 8th.

Post-exchange, the Sun becomes a powerful 3rd lord, a common factor in actors, musicians and other performers. Meanwhile, Venus goes to the 5th, which is a classic for creativity, drama and entertainment, not to mention an active love life. Note that, regardless of which planet occupies the 5th (pre- or post-exchange), there is the inescapable aspect of that powerful Saturn in the 8th. This perhaps explains why so many of her romances were frustrated by one circumstance or another – class divisions, drug addictions and scandal by association.

The real source of her success resides more in the multiple yogas in the angles – *lagnesh* Mercury in the 4th forming *Bhadra Yoga*, Jupiter in the 10th forming *Hamsa Yoga*, together forming two *Dharma Karma Adhipati Yogas*. Meanwhile the addition of the Moon/Mars pair adds *Chandra Mangala*, *Kesari* and a couple of *Dhana Yogas* to the mix.

The Sun is debilitated and aspected by a powerful Saturn, whereas Venus is ordinary and absent any affliction. Thus, Venus has the relative strength to function as control planet for this exchange. Its placement in the 3rd house is consistent with Bernhardt's fame as a performing artist.

Exchange of 3rd and 6th lords

Parashara says:

- *If the 3rd lord happens to be placed in the 6th house, the native will be inimical to his brother, be very wealthy, will have enmity with his maternal uncle, and will have love for his maternal aunt.* (BPHS 26:30)

- *If the 6th lord is situated in the 3rd house, the native will be given to anger, be bereft of courage, inimical to all his brothers, and will have disobedient servants.* (BPHS 26:63)

This is a *Dainya Parivartana Yoga* wherein the lords are in a mutual 4/10 relationship from *dusthana* and *upachaya* houses. Between these two difficult house lords, we expect the native to experience significant struggle in overcoming obstacles and competitors, paying the price perhaps in defeat or disease.

The native doesn't appear outwardly adventurous until challenged by competitors, at which time his courage emerges. He is capable of using his hands in some skilled way, which includes wielding them as weapons. His health is weak with respect to the lungs and digestion, but although initially poor, both improve over time. He may also have hearing problems, especially in the right ear.

His talents, of a technical or service nature, favor jobs in the medical, legal, military, police and security industries. His earnings gradually increase over time. He has little talent in the arts, and even though he might persevere, success will be hard-earned.

He has difficult relations with his brothers and sisters, some of whom may be involved in competitive sports. A younger sibling could be engaged in the purchase and sale of (stolen) vehicles or properties. His mother's siblings, who might have good jobs, reputation or status, also suffer misfortunes in life.

As an employee, skilled adversaries are much in evidence, and compete with him for job opportunities. As an employer, he has problems with staff – either through incompetence, theft or unreliability – leading to a situation of high turnover. His pets get lost, run away or are stolen.

Famous people with this yoga

Nat "King" Cole, musician; David Copperfield, illusionist; Otto Dietrich, Nazi press chief; Bob Fosse, dancer; James Garner, actor; L. Ron Hubbard, Scientologist; Ian McKellen, actor; Joe Montana, football player; Demi Moore, actress; Maximilian Robespierre, revolutionary; William Shatner, actor; Sirhan Sirhan, assassin; Edward Snowden, whistleblower; Dennis Wilson, musician; Christian Wirth, Nazi.

Case study

Edward Snowden, a former computer systems administrator for the CIA, became perhaps the world's most famous whistle-blower to date when he leaked information regarding the NSA's systemic monitoring of American citizens' emails, texts, and phone calls, as well as spying on countries deemed sympathetic to the USA. After fleeing the USA, Snowden was granted asylum in Russia, where he remains to this day. Since then, the US government has charged him with theft of government property and two counts of espionage, conviction on any of which charge could see him imprisoned for a decade.

Notwithstanding his fugitive status, Snowden's actions have changed the modern world. People, especially in America, no longer assume that their emails, texts and phone calls are kept private, and online business for domestic companies has suffered hugely. Although judgment on his status remains mixed in America, polls around the rest of the world regard Snowden to be more hero than traitor, and he has received numerous awards and accolades for his role in encouraging government transparency where it concerns the privacy of citizens.

Dubbed "a genius among geniuses" by his former colleagues, Snowden has an IQ of 145, speaks functional Chinese and Japanese, and at the height of his career was senior systems geek for the CIA.

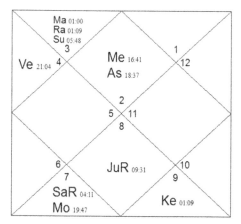

Venus in 3rd house Cancer exchanges with the Moon in 6th house Libra. Pre- or post-exchange, a powerful Saturn in the 6th influences both the 3rd and 6th houses and their lords, thus promising breaks in both limbs and employment.

This exchange between 3rd and 6th lords invokes their *upachaya* nature, for struggle and success. The 3rd is also a *kamasthana*, expressing a desire to do something, to summon courage and demonstrate prowess. The 6th is associated with service and employment but also the competitive spirit necessary to succeed in whatever *kshetra* is required – athletic field, courtroom or battlefield.

No matter whether *lagnesh* Venus or the Moon resides in the 6th house, we expect these themes to emerge in the life: competitive/combative nature, security work of some kind, potential litigation. As it turns out, Snowden enjoys martial arts, and joined the US reserve with the intention of fighting in Iraq but was discharged when he broke both legs during a training exercise.

He worked as both a security guard and analyst for the CIA and, ironically, has been accused of undermining US national security. His parents and siblings all worked for the federal government, two of them in a legal capacity. Despite his public persona, he is a soft-spoken vegetarian.

Since the Moon and Venus are both ordinary, there is no obvious control planet. Therefore, we might simply favor the 6th house, occupied by an exalted and retrograde Saturn. This is consistent with what he's known for: a security analyst turned whistle-blower, a digital Don Quixote now the object of governmental prosecution.

For a more complete analysis of his chart, see the Edward Snowden article on my website navamsa.com.

Exchange of 3rd and 7th lords

Parashara says:

- *Should the 3rd lord occupy the 7th house, the native will have aptitude for serving the King, he will not be happy during childhood but there is no doubt in it that he will get happiness at the end.* (BPHS 26:31)

- *If the 7th lord is situated in the 3rd house, the children of the native are subjected to (early) death. Sometimes a daughter is born, and a son may also remain living with great difficulty.* (BPHS 26:75)

This is a *Khala Parivartana Yoga* wherein the lords are in a mutual 5/9 relationship from *kama* houses. Because of this relationship, we expect a passionate approach to life that results in the ready fruition of artistic accomplishments and relationships.

The native is courageous, adventurous, willing to take risks, and intent on living an exciting and varied life. Talented in lovemaking, he may seek adventure through sexual relationships of an ephemeral nature. The exchange of two *kama* lords creates strong passions, which may strain a monogamous relationship. Either the native or his spouse has strong sexual drives that may not be fulfilled within the relationship.

The native is fond of travel and likely to form partnerships – business or personal – with foreigners. This combination favors careers in sales, marketing, and public relations. His siblings will be adventurous and well-traveled. He may share a special relationship with his sibling's children.

The spouse may be artistic or athletic, but willful and ill-tempered, such that occasional separations become likely. The spouse pursues foreign studies, and may share a mutual attraction with one of the native's siblings.

Famous people with this yoga

Tammy Faye Bakker, evangelist; Carla Bruni, model; Roger Daltrey, singer; John Wayne Gacy, serial killer; Francoise Gauquelin, statistician; Mel Gibson, actor; Lady Bird Johnson, US First Lady; Patty Hearst, publishing heiress; Jim Jarmusch, director; David Letterman, talk show host; Ed McMahon, TV host; Wendy Yoshimiro, political activist.

Case study

John Wayne Gacy, aka The Killer Klown, was a Chicago-area serial killer who during the 1970s sexually assaulted and murdered at least 33 teenage boys and young men. Most were buried under the cellar floor of his suburban home.

Gacy was brutalized by his father throughout his youth, sexually molested as a child by a family acquaintance, and later initiated homosexual contacts with several of his employees. He worked in a mortuary for a short period and at one time climbed naked into a coffin with a deceased young man.

While briefly serving time for sodomy, he was a model prisoner, and initiated a number of improvements in prison conditions. He was for a time the manager of three KFC stores and later a successful building contractor. A zealous social networker, he was an ardent Democrat and a president of the local Jaycees, whose dubious social activities at the time included prostitution and wife-swapping.

He was married twice, although his second wife divorced him for sexual impotency. He liked to entertain at children's parties wearing a signature clown costume. After being incarcerated, he began to paint, often featuring himself in costume. Some of his paintings sold for as much as $20,000, although many were later bought by victims' families in order to be burned.

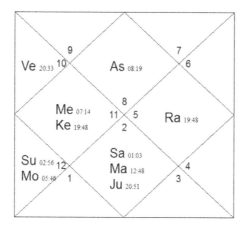

Venus in 3rd house Capricorn exchanges with Saturn in 7th house Taurus. The two are mutual friends exchanging via *kama* (desire) houses. Pre-exchange, Saturn enjoys *dig bala* in the 7th and forms one *Dharma Karma Adhipati Yoga* with *lagnesh* Mars, and another with 5th lord Jupiter.

Post-exchange, Venus in the 7th creates *karako bhavo nashto*, a situation that symbolically spoils relationships. Further note that, if Venus transfers its own degree position into the 7th house, it forms *graha yuddha* with Jupiter, a planetary war that afflicts both the object of affection (Jupiter as lord of the 5th) and the partner (Venus as lord of the 7th).

Pre-exchange, three *dusthana* lords (Saturn, Mars, Mercury) occupy the *kendras*. Post-exchange, three *dusthana* lords (Venus, Mars, Mercury) occupy the *kendras*. In either event, two associate with 5th lord Jupiter while simultaneously aspecting the *lagna*.

Interestingly enough, after years of engaging in forced homosexual rape, Gacy moved on to murder during the *bhukti* of Saturn, one of the players in this *Parivartana Yoga*.

While Venus is ordinary, Saturn's *dig bala* gives it the strength to function as control planet in this exchange. Its position in the 7th reflects the homicidal nature of his sexual obsessions.

Exchange of 3rd and 8th lords

Parashara says:

- *In case the 3rd lord is situated in the 8th house, the native will be a thief, will derive his livelihood from serving others, and will be killed by a king.* (BPHS 26:32)

- *In case the 8th lord is gone in the 3rd house, the native will be devoid of fraternal happiness, be indolent, be devoid of vigor, and without servants.* (BPHS 26:87)

This is a *Dainya Parivartana Yoga* wherein the lords are in a mutual 6/8 relationship from *dusthana* houses (the 3rd is a mild *dusthana*). Because of the relative positions of the participant planets, they are somewhat blind to each other, so that the yoga may not manifest on a public or conscious level, but in a more personal or unconscious manner.

The native is cautious, avoids risks, and has difficulty in fulfilling his desires. He may have secret adventures, either sexual or criminal in nature. He may be inclined to do things that transgress conventional laws or morals, such that his activities turn into misadventures.

He reveals a heightened level of sexual interest or activity, but also experiences stressful circumstances surrounding such activities, involving aberrations or trauma, eg, rape, incest, perversion, nymphomania or satyriasis, etc. The net effect is that he becomes sexually exhausted or debilitated over time.

He has health problems regarding his hearing, upper limbs and/or lungs. He is prone to mishaps, especially in the course of day-to-day travel. Longevity is poor. He engages in activities that are self-injurious, perhaps even life-threatening, sometimes verging on suicidal behavior.

Unless supported by other yogas or benefic aspects, this exchange suggests the native has difficulty expressing his artistic talents or athletic skills. On the other hand, he may have an interest or hidden talents in the occult or mystic arts.

His siblings are sickly, accident-prone and generally unlucky. They experience hardships in the form of emotional or physical trauma, financial reversals and premature demise.

Famous people with this yoga

Eva Gabor, actress; Max Klinger, artist; Vivien Leigh, actress; Michelangelo, Renaissance man; Louis Pasteur, scientist; Sri Bhagwan Rajneesh, guru; Boz Scaggs, musician; Robert Sherwood, playwright; Robert Stack, actor.

Case study

Sri Bhagwan Rajneesh was an Indian mystic and guru. Some describe his philosophy as a potpourri of counter-cultural ideas focusing on love and freedom, living for the moment, the importance of self, the mystery of life, individual responsibility for one's own destiny and the need to lose the ego, fear and guilt.

Critical of both contemporary Indian politics and religion, he was disparaged as much as admired. His ideas on sex, marriage, family and relationships contradicted traditional views, arousing anger and opposition. In India, he became known as the "sex guru" because his spiritual community practiced a form of sexual libertinism. His life was characterized by scandal and notoriety.

His lifestyle was lavish, with multiple mansions and 93 Rolls-Royces. For a period of time he and his followers resided in the USA, where he was dubbed the "Rolls-Royce guru." In America, he ran afoul of both the religious establishment and the tax authorities, was charged with 35 counts of conspiracy and fraud, briefly imprisoned and ultimately forced to leave the country.

He had impaired hearing in the right ear, suffered asthma and diabetes, and for a time took 60 mg Valium daily and was

addicted to nitrous oxide, under whose influence he dictated a
number of books. Over 650 books are attributed to him, mostly
transcriptions from his many public lectures, in which he was
acknowledged to be a spellbinding speaker.

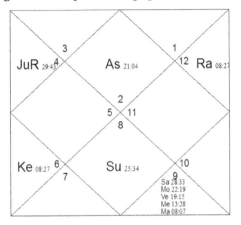

Jupiter in 3rd house Cancer exchanges with the Moon in 8th
house Sagittarius. Pre-exchange, Jupiter is strong, being both
exalted and retrograde, while the Moon is weak, being dark in
only the third *tithi* after the new moon.

Although the Moon participates in none of them, a massive
cluster of planets in the 8th generates seven *Dharma Karma
Adhipati Yogas* and two *Dhana Yogas*. This same concentration
of activity in the 8th house also fueled a major theme of
sexuality, which ultimately tainted his reputation.

Transposing Jupiter to the 8th creates a (virtual) *Viparita Yoga*,
with a full *mala* of *trik* lords (Venus, Jupiter and Mars) in a
trikasthana house. But since this is not a "pure" *Viparita* (ie, *trik*
lords segregated from innocent bystanders), it also has the side
effect of contaminating Mercury and Saturn, lords of 2nd/5th
and 9th/10th, respectively.

Thus, we see signs of substance abuse and poisoning (his US
ashram was found guilty of contaminating a neighboring
town's food supply), "wrong" (highly controversial) teaching,

rebellious acolytes (subversion from within his inner circle), unethical (questionable) conduct and outright clashes with government authorities, at one time seeking asylum but deemed *persona non grata* in every country where he sought refuge.

Whereas the Moon is dark, Jupiter is exalted and retrograde, making it the obvious choice for control planet of this exchange. Jupiter is "guru" in Sanskrit, hence its generic association with spiritual life. Its placement in the 3rd house also reminds us that Rajneesh was a prolific writer, both under his original name and his subsequent "relabeling" as Osho.

Exchange of 3rd and 9th lords

Parashara says:

- *If the 3rd lord happens to fall in the 9th house, the native is bereft of paternal happiness, makes fortunes through his wife, and enjoys the happiness of having sons, etc.* (BPHS 26:33)

- *If the 9th lord is placed in the 3rd house, the native will be blessed with fraternal bliss, be wealthy, virtuous and charming.* (BPHS 26:99)

This is a *Khala Parivartana Yoga* wherein the lords are in a mutual 7/7 relationship. Because this mutual aspect facilitates the individual's awareness of the exchange, the urge for integration is a fully conscious one.

The native has a strong desire for spiritual development but is frustrated in his efforts to make things happen as quickly as he would like. He has the courage to follow his principles, and takes up righteous causes. A bit of a fanatic, he tries too hard to convince others of his beliefs, and may get into trouble with the law through inflammatory writings or actions.

He relocates in order to pursue a higher education in the fine arts or the physical sciences. He travels a lot, both locally, and to foreign locales. He doesn't have any natural luck, but succeeds through his own efforts. He is talented in the literary arts, and may be a writer, a teacher or a media professional. Other potential occupations include columnists, editors and lawyers and pilots.

He enjoys good relations with his siblings, but a difficult relationship with his father. His siblings are religious, attached to their gurus, and travel to foreign countries for their higher education. The father is engaged in much day-to-day travel, and is artistic or athletic, but is likely to have a short life span.

Famous people with this yoga

Gianni Agnelli, industrialist; David Byrne, musician; Karen Carpenter, singer; Larry Csonka, football player; Tim Curry, actor; Robert Guccione, publisher; Erich Hartmann, ace fighter pilot; Waylon Jennings, singer; Katherine Mansfield, writer; Richard Nolle, astrologer; Don Schollander, Olympic swimmer; Mickey Spillane, writer; George Strait, singer; Tiger Woods, golfer.

Case study

Mickey Spillane was a prolific and successful writer, and his "hard-boiled" detective novels have sold over 225 million copies. An athletic man, he swam and played football in high school, while later in life he was a professional diver, a trampoline artist, a race car driver, a flight instructor and a WW2 fighter pilot.

He began his writing career creating scripts for comic books, including Captain America, Batman, Superman and Captain Marvel. Although his Mike Hammer series of hard-boiled detective novels outraged many critics of the day because of their overt descriptions of sex and violence, no less a literary icon than Ayn Rand publicly endorsed his work. Subsequent critics have come around to seeing poetry in his lean, muscular style of writing, and in 1985 he received the Edgar Allan Poe Grand Master Award for his body of work.

Spillane was an active Jehovah's Witness, was married three times, and died of pancreatic carcinoma at the age of 88.

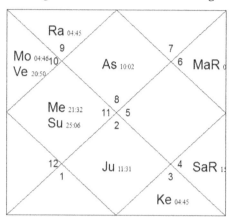

The Moon in 3rd house Capricorn exchanges with Saturn in 9th house Cancer. Saturn has strength as a retrograde, although the waning Moon is weak within four *tithis* of the new moon. Nevertheless, each planet aspects its own sign, thus granting their respective houses protection, meanwhile creating a strong theme of activity along the 3rd/9th axis.

Pre- or post-exchange, the Moon and Venus create one *Dharma Karma Adhipati Yoga*, while the Moon and Saturn create another. Although not a yoga *per se*, the Moon/Venus *sambandha* is a common factor seen in the charts of people of artistic temperament or profession.

3rd house themes are evident in his athleticism, physical prowess and daredevil character. 9th house themes came through as an interest in law, a devout religious practice, and his role as instructor, both in pilot training for the air force and in teaching writing at local colleges.

Whereas the Moon is dark, Saturn is retrograde, thus qualifying it as the control planet for this exchange. Its placement in the 9th reminds us of Spillane's success in publishing and teaching, as well as his lesser-known spiritual devotion.

Exchange of 3rd and 10th lords

Parashara says:

- *When the 3rd lord is placed in the 10th house, the native will have all kinds of happiness, and self-made wealth, and is apt to nurture wicked females.* (BPHS 26:34)

- *If the 10th lord is situated in the 3rd house, the native will enjoy happiness from brothers and servants, be valorous, virtuous, eloquent and truthful.* (BPHS 26:111)

This is a *Khala Parivartana Yoga* wherein the lords are in a mutual 6/8 relationship. These are both *upachaya* house lords, but their relationship makes it difficult for their owner to take full advantage of their partnership, so it takes considerable effort to yield significant results.

The native is talented in the fine arts, athletic activities, or one of the standard trades. Despite initial setbacks in his desires or ambitions, he eventually achieves success, thanks to the influence of *upachaya* lords, who are capable of conferring triumph over adversity, albeit after significant struggle.

He puts a lot of effort into his career, sometimes too aggressively, and could incur the displeasure of superiors and/or the public. He has the courage to take bold stands that generate publicity and visibility within his social circle. He may have an affair with someone at work.

He has special manual skills critical to his chosen profession, whether in the performing arts, sports or skilled trades. Due to occupational hazards, he may suffer injuries to his hearing, upper limbs, lungs, nerves or skin.

The person's siblings are helpful in pursuing his profession. One of the siblings may be employed in the arts, sports or skilled trades. Siblings are prone to accidents, setbacks and miscellaneous misfortunes in life.

Famous people with this yoga

William Jennings Bryan, politician; Michael Caine, actor; Albert Camus, writer; Lewis Carroll, logician/writer; Mia Farrow, actress; Betty Friedan, feminist; Linda Hunt, actress; Herman Kahn, strategist; Steve Miller, musician; Victoria Sackville-West, writer; Sepharial, occult journalist.

Case study

Mia Farrow is an actress, activist and former model. Her father was a film director, her mother actress Maureen O'Sullivan. She was raised Catholic and schooled by convent nuns for 13 years. Both older brothers died suddenly – one in a plane crash, the other by suicide.

She first gained notice in the television soap opera *Peyton Place*, from which she withdrew to marry Frank Sinatra when she was 21 and he was 50. After he discouraged her acting career, she became bored and they divorced after only two years of marriage. Her role in *Rosemary's Baby*, which won her a Golden Globe, catapulted her into stardom.

She visited India to study TM with Maharishi Mahesh Yogi at the same time as the Beatles. In 1970, she had an affair with and subsequently married conductor/composer André Previn with whom she had twins. They divorced in 1979.

Shortly thereafter, she began a relationship with Woody Allen, and from 1980 to 1992 starred in 13 of his movies. Their relationship collapsed when she discovered his interest in one of their adopted children, Korean-born Soon Yi. Thereafter, they split amid allegations and counter-accusations regarding various forms of abuse concerning other of their adopted children.

Since then, she's become a high-profile advocate for human rights in Africa, particularly children's rights, and has received several awards for her humanitarian work.

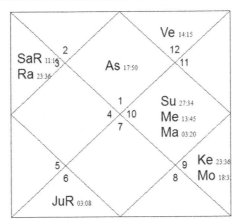

Saturn in 3rd house Gemini exchanges with Mercury in 10th house Capricorn. Saturn is strong, being retrograde, while Mercury associates with two fiery planets (both the Sun and Mars have *dig bala* in the 10th) without becoming combust. Neither planet participates in any other yoga.

Combinations involving the 3rd and 10th house lords are common among actors, musicians and other performers.

No matter where we look for siblings, trouble looms. Mercury is 3rd house lord (younger siblings), while Saturn is 11th house lord (older siblings). Pre- or post-exchange, one or the other is afflicted by the nodal axis or the malefic Sun/Mars pair (Mars is 8th lord), thus generating sorrow, especially for elder siblings.

Between the two of them, Mercury and Saturn rule all four *upachaya* houses – 3rd, 6th, 10th and 11th. Pre- or post-exchange, Mercury or Saturn also associate with command-and-control planets Sun and Mars in the 10th, thus provoking some sort of activism. This is most obvious in her humanitarian work, where she's been both aggressive and insistent on taking governments to task for their treatment of children.

While Mercury is merely ordinary, Saturn is retrograde, thus confirming it as the control planet in this exchange. Its placement in the 3rd house highlights her role as an actor.

Exchange of 3rd and 11th lords

Parashara says:

- *If the 3rd lord has gone into the 11th house, the native will always gain in trading, will be intelligent in spite of being illiterate, be adventurous, and will serve others.* (BPHS 26:35)

- *If the 11th lord be situated in the 3rd house, the native will be skillful in all jobs, wealthy, be blessed with fraternal bliss, and sometimes may incur gout pains.* (BPHS 26:123)

This is a *Khala Parivartana Yoga* wherein the lords are in a mutual 5/9 relationship from *upachaya* and *kama* houses. Because of this pattern, the powerful combination of desire and effort is accompanied by a certain degree of good fortune, thus yielding commensurate results.

The native has the courage to address large assemblies, and may act as a spokesperson for an association or society. He is talented in entertaining large groups of people, through speaking or performing. He takes part in a group adventure, and is a member of a musical group or performing arts troupe. He may be ambidextrous, and has a good musical ear.

After a period of struggle, his ambitions are ultimately fulfilled and his gains accumulate gradually. He is a natural trader who makes money by taking calculated risks. Alternatively, he earns money through the arts, writing or technical trades.

He also gains wealth through his siblings, who support his hopes and ambitions. His younger siblings pursue foreign travels. He has a close relationship with his sibling's children. He has many friends who are treated as part of the family.

Famous people with this yoga

Helen Gurley Brown, publisher; Chrissie Hynde, singer; Jayne Mansfield, actress; Marion March, astrologer; Emperor Maximilian I, German royalty; Jimmy Page, musician; Carlo Ponti, producer; Kelly Quinn, psychic; John Rechy, writer; Keith Richards, musician; Telly Savalas, actor; Jo Jo Starbuck, Olympic skater; Bobby Womack, musician.

Case study

Keith Richards is a musician, singer and songwriter, an original member of the world's most enduring rock band, the Rolling Stones. Fellow musicians note that, while most bands follow their drummer, the Stones have no choice but to follow helmsman Richards.

Richards is both a traditionalist, favoring acoustic blues, and an innovator, using 5-stringed electric guitars with open tuning. *Rolling Stone* magazine credited him for "rock's greatest single body of riffs" on guitar and ranked him 4th on its list of 100 best guitarists.

Long defying Top 10 lists of who'll die next, Richards is an archetype of a rock star's gypsy lifestyle. One journalist labeled him with Lord Byron's epithet – "mad, bad, and dangerous to know." Another said he's "a capering streak of living gristle who ought to be exhibited as a warning to youth of what drugs can do to you even if you're lucky enough not to choke on your own vomit."

Richards, who's been frank about his drug abuse, including heroin addiction and blood-cleansing in Swiss clinics, has been tried on drug-related charges five times.

An avid reader with a strong interest in WW2 history, he owns an extensive library. A 2010 article revealed he yearns to be a librarian. Co-written with a journalist, Richards' memoir *Life* was released in 2010, following a US publisher's advance of US $7.3 million.

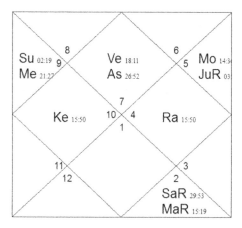

The Sun in 3rd house Sagittarius exchanges with Jupiter in 11th house Leo. The two are mutual friends in *kama* and *upachaya* houses. The pre-exchange Sun and Mercury form a *Dhana Yoga*. Jupiter is strong, being retrograde, and forms *Kesari Yoga* with a relatively bright Moon.

Whether before or after the Sun/Jupiter exchange, (inflammatory) Mars still aspects both the 3rd house and its lord Jupiter. From most current photos, it appears that Richards' hands are becoming arthritic.

3rd house themes are revealed through his guitar prowess, songwriting talents and love of books. Note that the 3rd/11th exchange involves the two houses that rule the right and left hands, respectively. Interestingly, another fabled rock guitarist, Jimmy Page, also has a 3rd/11th exchange.

The 11th house theme has played out in "group work", a huge income, an iconic social profile as a rock star, ongoing dedication to fellow musicians, and a collection of guitars that numbers over 3000.

Whereas the Sun is merely ordinary, Jupiter is retrograde and therefore emerges as the control planet for this exchange. Its placement in the 11th highlights Richards' primary role in a group wherein he is universally acknowledged as the helmsman of the world's greatest rock 'n' roll band.

Exchange of 3rd and 12th lords

Parashara says:

- *In the event of the 3rd lord being placed in the 12th house, the native will spend his wealth in evil deeds, his father will be cruel, and the native becomes fortunate through his wife.* (BPHS 26:36)

- *If the 12th lord is placed in the 3rd house, the native will be devoid of fraternal bliss, will have hatred for other people, and will promote self-nourishment or be self-centered.* (BPHS 26:135)

This is a *Dainya Parivartana Yoga* wherein the lords are in a mutual 4/10 relationship from *dusthana* houses. There is tension and lack of easy rapport in situations representing this yoga, especially sexual adventures or distant travels.

The native is interested in spiritual liberation and self-improvement, but lacks the courage of his convictions to make a daily discipline of his practice. Instead, he may perform mean acts in secrecy or in a subversive manner. He may receive sexual initiation from a sibling or neighbor, and thereafter has an unconventional attitude towards sexuality.

He is physically restless, spends money on unwholesome adventures in foreign places, and writes about his experiences. He often regrets (the 12th house is hindsight) things he said or did, and should be careful of things put in writing, which may come back to haunt him.

He has health problems related to his hearing, upper limbs and lungs. He will make frequent trips to a day clinic. Coordination of hands or fingers is poor and, in some cases, may entail the total dysfunction or loss of digital control.

Unless supported by other factors, this exchange suggests the native has neither artistic talents nor athletic abilities, but has gifts in the occult arts. He may have clairaudient faculties, although the "voices" he hears are not always reliable.

He incurs expenses on behalf of his siblings, who are sick, unlucky or dispossessed of their domestic comforts. Siblings experience frequent change and dislocation in their professional lives, or isolation in the form of hospitalization, imprisonment, or foreign residence.

Famous people with this yoga

Prince Albert, British royalty; Peter Bogdanovitch, director; Lloyd Bridges, actor; Rita Mae Brown, writer; Paul Cézanne, artist; Jean Chretien, politician; John Densmore, musician; Richard Dreyfuss, actor; Julie Harris, actress; King Henry IV, French royalty; Hal Holbrook, actor; MacGregor Mathers, occultist; Vance Packard, writer; Gregory Peck, actor; James Plunkett, football player; Lily Pons, opera singer; Edward G. Robinson, actor; Britney Spears, singer; Barbra Streisand, entertainer.

Case study

Paul Cézanne was a French artist and post-Impressionist painter who paved the transition from 19th-century artistic conceptions to a radically different art in the 20th century. His explorations of geometric simplification and optical phenomena inspired Picasso and others to experiment with more complex views of the same subject and eventually to the fracturing of form.

His father, a successful banker, provided Cézanne a financial security unavailable to most of his contemporaries and eventually left him a large inheritance. Cézanne was married with one son, but the marriage was stormy, with frequent separations.

Cézanne's works were rejected numerous times by the official Salon in Paris and ridiculed by art critics when exhibited with the Impressionists. Yet during his lifetime he was considered a master by younger artists who visited his studio in Aix-en-Provence.

Despite later public recognition and financial success, Cézanne chose to work in increasing artistic isolation, spending long periods as a virtual recluse. He was rude, shy, angry, and given to depression. During his so-called "dark period", his work included erotic and violent subject matter.

Caught in a downpour one day, he continued working in the field for two hours before going home; the next day, he was put to bed, but never left it, dying of pneumonia.

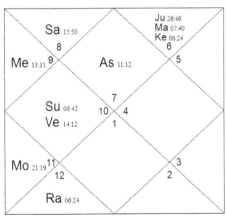

Mercury in 3rd house Sagittarius exchanges with Jupiter in 12th house Virgo. Neither planet contributes to the formation of any other constructive yoga. Pre- and post-exchange, both planets remain afflicted. Mercury is aspected by Mars, and hemmed by the Sun and Saturn. Jupiter is associated with Mars and the Rahu-Ketu axis.

Given the close association of Mars on that axis, versus the "oscillating" contribution of Jupiter, we're inclined to regard the *Kala Sarpa* configuration as more of a *dosha* than a yoga, with all its associated misfortunes.

3rd house themes are revealed through his novel technique of painting, using planes of color and small brush strokes built up to form complex fields of view. His early paintings also reflected 12th house themes of sexual obsession, repressed anger, violence, pain and frustration. Although ultimately the toast of Parisian art society, Cézanne was a recluse for much of his life, preferring the solitude of country living and the company of farmers and peasants.

Both Mercury and Jupiter are ordinary, although Jupiter is the more afflicted of the two. Therefore, Mercury has the relative strength to function as control planet for this exchange, its 3rd house placement reflecting his technical mastery of his art.

Exchanges Involving the 4th House Lord

Exchange of 4th and 5th lords

Parashara says:

- *If the 4th lord is situated in the 5th house, the native will be happy, be favorite of all, devotee of Lord Vishnu, virtuous, honorable, and will possess self-earned wealth.* (BPHS 26:41)

- *If the 5th lord occupies the 4th house, the native will be happy, having the blessing of maternal happiness, wealth and intelligence, and be a king or a minister or a preceptor.* (BPHS 26:52)

This is a *Maha Parivartana Yoga* (also a *Dharma Karma Adhipati Yoga*) wherein the lords are in a mutual 2/12 relationship. The combination of a *kendra* and *trikona* lord assures that fortune goes hand in hand with commensurate effort.

The native is intelligent and gets a good education. Possibly as a result of his mother's influence, he is spiritually inclined, studies scriptures or classical works, and attempts to pass on similar training to his own children. He takes pleasure in riding horses or vehicles. His home is a place of learning and contains a good library.

He studies or pursues a career in mining, oceanography, agriculture, civil engineering, education, psychology, or social work. He gains through government, the field of education, real estate investments, or trade in vehicles of one kind or another. He may teach executives, government employees or children. He could be employed as a writer-in-residence.

His mother is interested in religion or education. Her finances are secure. His children are well settled in life and a source of happiness for him, even though they may experience loss or significant changes in life. Children may travel abroad or immigrate.

Famous people with this yoga

Pedro Almodovar, director; Lisa Bonet, actress; Richard Carpenter, musician; Pablo Casals, cellist; Derek Clayton, track & field star; Keith Emerson, musician; Greta Garbo, actress; Bobby Hull, hockey player; Klaus Kinski, actor; Dean Martin, entertainer; Joni Mitchell, singer; Bill Moyers, journalist; Joachim Von Ribbentrop, diplomat; Henri Rousseau, artist; Carlos Santana, musician; Ted Turner, entrepreneur.

Case study

Ted Turner, former media mogul turned environmental philanthropist, is among the top 300 wealthiest people in the USA. He inherited the family billboard business after his father committed suicide. Early in his career he invested in radio stations and later switched to TV stations, then to cable networks, founding CNN in 1980.

He helped reinvent interest in professional wrestling, and is the owner of the Atlanta Braves and Atlanta Hawks. A political activist, he's fought for environmental causes, population control and nuclear containment, and in 1998 donated $1 billion to the United Nations.

Turner has been married and divorced three times, and has five children. In a 2012 interview with Piers Morgan, Turner admitted he had four girlfriends, which he acknowledged was complicated but easier than being married.

He has received multiple awards in recognition for his civic work, named Humanist of the Year in 1990, *Time* magazine's Man of the Year in 1991, and many other accolades.

In 2008, Turner said on PBS that if steps weren't taken to address global warming, people would die and "the rest of us will be cannibals." Indeed, Turner's penchant for controversial statements over the years earned him the nicknames "The Mouth of the South" and "Captain Outrageous."

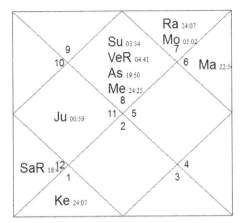

Jupiter in 4th house Aquarius exchanges with Saturn in 5th house Pisces. Saturn is strong (retrograde) in mutual aspect with Mars, thus creating a *Dharma Karma Adhipati Yoga*.

Post-exchange, Saturn, the *karaka* for undeveloped land, moves into the house signifying property. Indeed, Turner is one of America's largest private landowners, owning 15 ranches with a total of approximately 2,000,000 acres. He also owns the largest herd of (50,000) bison in the world.

4th house themes are also evident in his original passion for the Greek classics at university, and his command of racing yachts. He successfully defended America's Cup against Australia in 1977 and holds four "Yachtsman of the Year" awards. 5th house themes include his ownership of multiple sports franchises and TV networks.

Ascendant lord *bhumikaraka* Mars is also involved in a second *Parivartana Yoga* with Mercury in the 1st, whose exchange itself constitutes a *Dhana Yoga*. As noted earlier, only 3% of the population has two mutual receptions in their charts.

Whereas Jupiter is merely ordinary, Saturn is retrograde, and thus becomes the control planet in this exchange. Its 5th house placement is consistent with Turner's empire having been built on sports franchises and entertainment networks.

Exchange of 4th and 6th lords

Parashara says:

- *In the event of the 4th lord falling in the 6th house, the native will be devoid of maternal happiness. He will be given to wrath, be a thief and a man of questionable character, self-willed and vicious.* (BPHS 26:42)

- *In case the 6th lord is situated in the 4th house, the native will be devoid of maternal happiness, intelligent, a tale bearer, jealous, fickle-minded and very rich.* (BPHS 26:64)

This is a *Dainya Parivartana Yoga* wherein the lords are in a mutual 3/11 relationship. Because of the dynamic between the participant planets (*kendra* lord and *trik* lord) results will come only grudgingly after a period of tribulation.

The native's values are tainted, and there's a tendency to take an aggressive or avaricious approach to dealing with others, such that conflict in the home or the community is likely. He experiences health problems via rheumatism or weakness of the heart.

His home is often in a state of renovation or repair. Property and real estate are sources of disputes, leading to lawsuits over ownership, disagreements with tenants, houses requiring repair. Vehicles are another source of problems, being in a state of disrepair or involving him in accident or injury.

He must work hard to achieve an education, during which competition is severe. He's strongly interested in healing, and has an intuitive approach to diagnosis. Although there are interruptions or obstacles in completing a degree, he acquires an education in medicine, military studies, law enforcement, veterinary science or environmental studies.

He has a great affinity for animals and works as a vet, animal trainer or animal rights advocate. He works at home, or spends so much time at work that his office is like a home away from home.

His mother has health problems and is a source of worry or sorrow. If not mentally or physically ill, she's at odds with the native, causing disagreements and enmity. She takes many short journeys. Her siblings have good incomes.

Famous people with this yoga

Ned Beatty, actor; Eric Burdon, singer; Sandy Dennis, actress; Joan Didion, writer; Bob Dylan, musician; George Eliot, writer; Naomi Judd, singer; Stacy Keach, actor; Henri Matisse, artist; Nancy Mitford, writer; Gwyneth Paltrow, actress; Rusty Schweickart, astronaut; Upton Sinclair, writer; Luchino Visconti, director.

Case study

Bob Dylan, musician and songwriter, has written over 300 songs, selling 100 million records over a career spanning 50 years. Defying existing pop music conventions, his work incorporated political, social, philosophical and literary influences in a style once described as surreal talking blues.

Shy, moody, careless of his health, scared by fame, immaterial but shrewd about money, he was a profound intellectual who, despite mixed reviews in his early years, was supported by peers Joan Baez and Johnny Cash.

After a serious motorcycle accident that broke his neck and almost killed him, he went into seclusion for eight years before touring again. In later years, his health deteriorated. In 1997, he was hospitalized with a life-threatening heart infection.

He was married twice, with six children, and has been the object of a couple of paternity suits.

He has received multiple awards, including a Golden Globe and a Grammy for Lifetime Achievement. Despite his loyal fan base, his overall output has been spotty. One critic characterized his singing as "a catarrhal death rattle." Live performances have been irregular, and studio productions criticized for sloppiness. One of his films was judged an "incoherent mess."

A 2007 study of US legal briefs found his lyrics quoted by judges and lawyers more than any other songwriter, the most widely cited line being "you don't need a weatherman to know which way the wind blows."

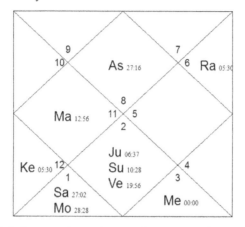

Mars in 4th house Aquarius exchanges with Saturn in 6th house Aries. Saturn is debilitated but forms a *Dharma Karma Adhipati Yoga* with the Moon.

Post-exchange, Mars from the 6th house aspects its own sign in the ascendant, thus fueling the aggressive stance that marked so much of his early work, both in personal style and socio-political alliances.

4th house themes are evident in his populist appeal and his very strong fan base. The 4th/6th exchange, although not a classic for vehicular accidents, provides the setup for related injuries. Heart ailments are to be expected, given the exchange of two malefics across these houses, and especially considering Saturn's debilitation.

6th house themes have emerged via health problems, litigations (divorce and paternity suits) and strong alliance with labor movements of the 60s.

Whereas Saturn is debilitated, Mars is merely ordinary, a weak endorsement for it to be control planet for this exchange. Its placement in the 4th house does reflect, however, his heart ailments, vehicular problems, and fiercely loyal fan base.

Exchange of 4th and 7th lords

Parashara says:

- *If the 4th lord has gone in the 7th house, the native will be highly learned in various branches of knowledge, will be apt to leave his paternal property, and will be akin to the dumb in an assembly.* (BPHS 26:43)

- *In case the 7th lord is situated in the 4th house, the wife of the native will not remain under his control. He will himself be truthful, intelligent and religious, and he will suffer from dental diseases.* (BPHS 26:76)

This is a *Maha Parivartana Yoga* wherein the lords are in a mutual 4/10 relationship from *kendra* houses. With this pattern between *kendra* lords, this yoga implies a certain degree of community outreach, intertwined in the realm of relationships, moral values and happiness.

The native has a strong desire for education or spiritual liberation, and leaves his home in pursuit of it. He gets an education in sales, marketing, public relations, foreign trade, or matters relating to partnerships, contracts and agreements.

He is happy at home, and takes pride in his property and/or vehicle(s). He owns a foreign car, or is involved in the trade of foreign cars. His happiness depends to a considerable degree on the quality (and/or quantity) of his relationships.

His spouse is very independent, and difficult to contain within the normal confines of a marriage. The spouse will have a good professional reputation and be engaged in an occupation involving real estate, vehicles, education, or psychology. The spouse is comfortable and happy, although perhaps something of a workaholic.

His mother is extroverted, educated and well-traveled. She may also be involved in the purchase and sale of properties.

Famous people with this yoga

Gregg Allman, musician; Maya Angelou, poet; Giovanni Falcone, anti-Mafia judge; Henry Ford Jr., entrepreneur; Michael J. Fox, actor; Tom Hanks, actor; Odetta, singer; Alan Oken, astrologer; Louis Pasteur, scientist; Leon Russell, musician; William Shatner, actor; Grace Slick, singer; Paul Theroux, writer; Jack Valenti, director; Dwight Yoakam, singer; Bernard Zuckerman, chess grandmaster.

Case study

Maya Angelou was a much-loved American sage, poet, performing artist and author of over 12 best-selling books.

When she was three, her parents divorced and she was raised by her paternal grandparents. At age eight she was raped by her mother's boyfriend, who was subsequently killed by her outraged uncles. Maya withdrew into isolation and remained mute for five years, during which time she developed a love of books.

A devotee of dance, she performed in nightclubs and off-Broadway productions. She worked as a cook and prostitute. She wrote songs, worked as an editor for civil rights causes (with Martin Luther King and Malcolm X), wrote and produced a TV series and published her memoirs to public acclaim.

Multilingual as well as multi-talented, Angelou spoke six languages. She was married three times and had one child. She was a striking figure, standing six feet tall and wearing signature vibrant colors.

She received over 50 honorary doctorates and in 1983 was named by *Ladies' Home Journal* among the One Hundred Most Influential American Women. Bill Clinton invited her to write the 1993 inaugural poem for his administration.

In later years she was active on the lecture circuit, giving as many as 80 talks a year. She was respected as a spokesperson for black people and women, and her works have been considered a defense of Black culture.

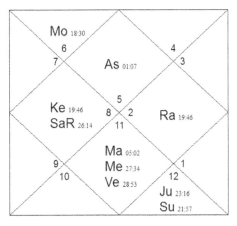

Saturn in 4th house Scorpio exchanges with Mars in 7th house Aquarius. Saturn is strong (retrograde) but afflicted by the Rahu-Ketu axis. Mars is ordinary but in the company of benefics. Its association with Venus creates a *Dharma Karma Adhipati Yoga*, while with Mercury it creates two *Dhana Yogas*.

Post-exchange, Saturn in the 7th forms *Sasha Yoga*, gains *dig bala*, and joins two natural friends. In moving to the 4th, Mars forms *Ruchaka Yoga*. But no matter whether before or after exchange, four malefics continue to occupy the *kendras*, signifying a life of struggle.

4th house themes played out in domestic hardship and emotional turmoil, including depression.

7th house themes emerged via troubled relationships, including violence. At the same time, her role as a spokesperson for her people carried her fame far and wide.

Whereas Mars is merely ordinary, Saturn is retrograde, and therefore qualifies as control planet in this exchange. Its position in the 4th may seem difficult to rationalize until we reflect that the 4th represents one's constituency, fans, tribe, and people. As such, Angelou was a spokesperson for an entire culture.

Exchange of 4th and 8th lords

Parashara says:

- *When the 4th lord happens to be placed in the 8th house, the native will be devoid of domestic and other comforts, will not get much paternal happiness, and be equal to a neuter.* (BPHS 26:44)

- *When the 8th lord occupies the 4th house, the native will be deprived of his mother, and there can be no doubt in it that he will be devoid of a house, lands, and happiness, and will be a betrayer of friends.* (BPHS 26:88)

This is a *Dainya Parivartana Yoga* wherein the lords are in a mutual 5/9 relationship from *moksha* houses. The native may appear unconventional, seeking catharsis via escape from the home, maternal influence, community values or conventional morality.

His state of happiness is disturbed by unfortunate events. His mind is subject to addictions and obsessions, so he gets drawn into negative thinking and behavior. He suffers heartbreak, figuratively via happiness destroyed, or literally in the form of a heart ailment.

His mother has difficulties, including accidents, surgeries, death in the family, and general misfortune. Nevertheless, she gains through speculation or games of chance.

His domestic life is in a constant state of upheaval, with many changes of residence, renovations due to accidents, and problems with property insurance. In a similar vein, vehicles prove problematic.

He has deep sexual feelings, and may receive an education or pursue a path that entails secret teachings regarding sexuality. His morality may be perverted, such that he commits crimes of conscience, especially of a sexual nature. He keeps aspects of his personality hidden, and may at times go into hiding.

He has a strong intuition to follow a path of *moksha*, and foregoes many creature comforts, giving up property and inheritance in order to pursue his spiritual liberation.

He has difficulty finishing his education, experiencing breaks in studies, and changes of direction. He acquires knowledge in the fields of psychology, parapsychology and the occult, and may write about such subjects. Suitable professions include research and investigation, banking and insurance, renovation and rehabilitation, undertaking and estate planning.

Famous people with this yoga

Susan Atkins, cult killer; Jean Auel, writer; Bernardo Bertolucci, director; Beau Bridges, actor; John Denver, musician; Aretha Franklin, singer; André Gide, writer; Rex Harrison, actor; Hans Holzer, occult writer; Jay Leno, talk show host; Kate Millett, feminist; Spike Milligan, writer/director; Tip O'Neill, politician; J. Henri Poincaré, mathematician; Kiefer Sutherland, actor; John Travolta, actor; Maurice Utrillo, artist; King Vidor, producer.

Case study

Jay Leno is an American comedian and talk show host. Mildly dyslexic, he majored in speech therapy during college studies, and earned his living by performing his comedy act at night clubs.

Leno exemplified clean humor, as opposed to vulgar jokes which others told about blacks, gays and women, hiding prejudice behind comedy. He struggled for years to make it, watching contemporaries advance in their careers before he succeeded Johnny Carson as host of *The Tonight Show*.

He has a fleet of over 169 classic cars and 117 motorcycles. He loves to repair mechanical things and has said that if he hadn't made it as a comedian, he would have become an auto mechanic.

After giving testimony in the 2005 trial of Michael Jackson over allegations of child molestation, Leno was banned from telling jokes about Jackson, but exploited a legal loophole so other stand-in comedians could take the stage and crack jokes. During the 2007-08 writers' strike, he was accused of violating guidelines by writing his own monologue.

After orchestrating his "retirement" in 2008 from *The Tonight Show* in favor of Conan O'Brien, Leno and NBC reneged on the arrangement, much to the chagrin of O'Brien and his fans. As a result, Leno was viewed as a bad guy and seriously maligned in the press.

~

The Sun in 4th house Aries exchanges with Mars in 8th house Leo. The two mutual friends are both strong – the Sun exalted, Mars retrograde. Mars is part of a 5-planet complex in the 2nd/8th house axis that involves an impressive array of yogas: *Chandra Mangala*, a *Dharma Karma Adhipati Yoga* with each of Venus and Saturn, and a *Dhana Yoga* with each of them again.

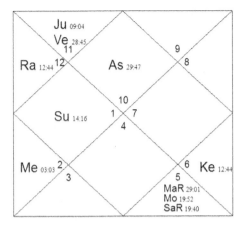

4th house themes are evident in his vast collection of vehicles, while the 8th house theme arises from his repair and restoration work. This is as good an example as any by which to remind readers that, although an individual may be famous for one thing, an exchange pattern in the chart may reveal something entirely different, more personal than professional.

For instance, consider Leno's dubious ethics, which are muddied by the exchange of 4th and 8th lords. Despite being a proponent of clean jokes for the sake of his fans and the public, Leno has always taken care of #1. His exploitation of a legal loophole during the embargo on Michael Jackson jokes, his violation of the writers' strike guidelines, and his reversal on surrendering the host slot of *The Tonight Show* to O'Brien all point to someone who has a hard time letting go.

Whereas Mars is just ordinary, the Sun is exalted and therefore qualifies as the control planet for this exchange. Its placement in the 4th, however mundane, evokes his great love of cars.

Exchange of 4th and 9th lords

Parashara says:

- *If the 4th lord is situated in the 9th house, the native will be loved by one and all, be a devotee of God, virtuous, honorable and blessed with every kind of happiness.* (BPHS 26:45)

- *If the 9th lord is situated in the 4th house, the native will be endowed with the happiness of having houses and conveyances, will have all kinds of wealth, and be devoted to his mother.* (BPHS 26:100)

This is a *Maha Parivartana Yoga* (also a *Dharma Karma Adhipati Yoga*) wherein the lords are in a mutual 6/8 relationship. Although this person may experience moral dilemmas, especially within a marital relationship, he eventually resolves his difficulties by deferring to his moral compass.

The native will have high moral standards, and be a model of ethical behavior for those among his circle. Such a person always follows his higher conscience, for his desire is to approach God. He is respected, achieves a certain reputation within his milieu, and enjoys the comforts of his status.

His parents are spiritual, well-educated and well-traveled. His father experiences setbacks in life. His mother is vulnerable to common ailments or disease.

He benefits through real estate, vehicles, domestic articles and things beneath the ground. The home displays religious objects, or a portion of the home is dedicated to a spiritual practice. Alternatively, the home is located near a religious establishment, or has the appearance of such an establishment.

He is fond of foreign travel, and pursues an advanced degree during the course of his travels. He is adept in philosophy, law and spiritual subjects. He is close to his teacher or guru, and may himself become a teacher.

Famous people with this yoga

Willy Brandt, politician; Keith Haring, artist; Kevin Kline, actor; Charles Lamb, essayist; Andreas Papandreou, politician; Simone Signoret, actress; Aaron Spelling, producer; Lana Turner, actress; Gianni Versace, designer.

Case study

Lana Turner, an American film and television actress, was discovered at age 16. With over 50 films to her credit, most of her roles were due to her elegance, poise and the ability to project promiscuous sensuality.

She was the only daughter of teenaged parents who struggled to make ends meet. Her father was murdered when she was nine. Her mother worked 80 hours a week as a beautician.

Her role in *The Postman Always Rings Twice* established her as a serious actor. She later received an Academy Award nomination for her role in the movie *Peyton Place*.

Turner's personal life was as melodramatic as her films. She was married eight times (twice to the same man), and always in and out of sexual escapades. She once commented, "My goal was to have one husband and seven children, but it turned out the other way around."

She had one abortion and several miscarriages, made more than one suicide attempt, and was involved in several lawsuits. Her daughter stabbed one of Lana's lovers to death.

She smoked and drank heavily, had throat cancer twice, and at one time weighed only 95 pounds. After her final divorce in 1969 she claimed she had no desire to marry again and was celibate for the rest of her life. She stopped drinking, ate organic food, and embraced a spiritual life.

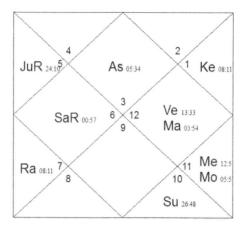

Saturn in Virgo 4th exchanges with Mercury in Aquarius 9th. Saturn is strong because retrograde. Saturn forms a *Viparita Yoga* with Mars and Venus, since all three are *trik* lords in *sambandha*, yet involve no other planets.

Lagnesh Mercury opposes Jupiter to form two *Dharma Karma Adhipati Yogas*, and associates with the Moon for a *Dhana Yoga*.

Whether pre-exchange from the 4th or post-exchange from the 9th, Saturn continues to aspect the 6th, thus contributing to Turner's frequent health problems.

4th/9th house themes (note the 6/8 relationship) played out in struggles for both parents. Legal disputes regarding her estate might also be read into this, since she left her maid the bulk of her fortune despite a legal challenge from her daughter.

The 9th house theme of spiritual pursuits really only emerged in her twilight years after she had exhausted her material side. In 1980, Turner had what she referred to as a "spiritual awakening" and became a devout Roman Catholic.

Whereas Mercury is ordinary, Saturn is retrograde, thus making it the control planet for this exchange. Its placement in the 4th, from where it aspects the *lagna* and forms a complex *Viparita Yoga* with Mars and Venus, speaks to her emotional discontent and the general unhappiness of her life.

Exchange of 4th and 10th lords

Parashara says:

- *Should the 4th lord occupy the 10th house, the native will enjoy royal honors, be an alchemist, be extremely pleased, will have pleasures, and will be conqueror of his five senses.* (BPHS 26:46)

- *Should the 10th lord be situated in the 4th house, the native will enjoy happiness, be devoted to his mother and be interested in her welfare, will have conveyances, lands and houses, be virtuous and wealthy.* (BPHS 26:112)

This is a *Maha Parivartana Yoga* wherein the lords are in a mutual 7/7 relationship from *kendra* houses. Note that the *sambandha* between these two lords in mutual aspect further strengthens each other's significations.

The native's moral standards are made known within his social milieu, such that his ethical conduct becomes a subject for public scrutiny and commentary. On balance, his standards are consistent with those of the public at large. He is interested and involved in politics. He may identify strongly with his community, his constituency, his country – and vice versa – thus qualifying him for a spokesperson or leadership role.

His mother is successful in business, enjoys an excellent reputation within her social circle and may be well-travelled. However, she may not enjoy a long life span.

He gets an education related to business, eg, degrees in commerce or finance, or a license in real estate. He is inclined to a career in agriculture, mining, construction, hotel management, car dealerships, real estate, etc, but also professions such as education, architecture, psychology, social work and government.

His home may be used as his place of business, for significant social functions, or enjoy some status as a heritage site.

Famous people with this yoga

Napoleon Bonaparte I, Emperor; Bernadette Brady, astrologer; José Ferrer, actor; Jean Luc Godard, director; Guglielmo Marconi, scientist; Michel de Nostradamus, prophet; Auguste Renoir, artist; Ivana Trump, socialite; Kurt Waldheim, politician.

Case study

Ivana Trump is a former world-class skier with a Master's degree. Born in Czechoslovakia, she immigrated to Canada and for a time was a model for several top fur companies. She moved to New York to help promote the 1976 Montreal Olympics and there met Donald Trump.

She became heavily involved in Trump's extensive hotel empire, was appointed Vice President of Interior Design, and awarded Hotelier of the Year in 1990. After Donald Trump's affair with Marla Maples became public, Ivana sued for divorce, pursuing a larger settlement than had been outlined in their pre-nuptial agreement. Aside from her marriage to Trump, there had been one husband earlier, and two later, but none that lasted.

Subsequent to her divorce from Trump, she developed lines of clothing, fashion jewelry, and beauty products that have been successfully sold through television shopping channels. She has also written several bestselling books, and penned a divorce advice column.

~

The Sun in 4th house Aquarius exchanges with Saturn in 10th house Leo. The two are not only in exchange but aspecting each other's own sign, which tends to further highlight the themes of their respective houses. The fact that they're both malefics and mutual enemies lends tension to that age-old dilemma of home versus career, private life versus public.

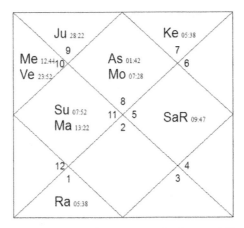

Pre-exchange, the Sun and Saturn each form a *Dharma Karma Adhipati Yoga* with *lagnesh* and *bhumikaraka* Mars. Saturn is strong because retrograde. Post-exchange, the Sun gains *dig bala*.

Since both exchange planets continue to interact with *lagnesh* Mars, which disposits the Moon in the ascendant, this explains Ivana's formidable and feisty personality.

4th house themes are very evident in her career as hotelier, while 10th house themes are equally dominant as socialite, spokesperson and columnist.

Whereas the Sun is ordinary, Saturn is retrograde, making it the control planet for this exchange. Although she's enjoyed success in her own right, Ivana's essential claim to fame was as a socialite, which is reflected in Saturn's position in the 10th.

Exchange of 4th and 11th lords

Parashara says:

- *In case the 4th lord has gone in the 11th house, the native will be obsessed with fear of secret disease, be liberal, virtuous, charitable and helpful to others.* (BPHS 26:47)

- *In case the 11th lord is situated in the 4th house, the native will have gains from maternal relatives, will make pilgrimages, and will possess happiness of house and lands.* (BPHS 26:124)

This is a *Maha Parivartana Yoga* wherein the lords are in a mutual 6/8 relationship. Because of this dynamic, the native may experience some struggle in the realization of his happiness, hopes and dreams, but ultimately his ambitions are fulfilled.

The native enjoys financial gains from his mother. Although she experiences many setbacks and reversals in life, including accidents and surgeries, she is often engaged in social networks and enjoys profitable ventures. She may enjoy easy access to capital.

He shares his home and vehicles with his friends, who are a source of comfort and happiness. His friends are educated, interested in a spiritual life, and have good ethical standards.

His elder siblings get a good education and are involved in careers such as teaching, real estate, property management, and agriculture. However, his elder siblings may be prone to common ailments or disease.

He establishes goals for his education, and is successful in completing them as per his plans. Money spent on education turns out to be a good investment, and prepares him for success in the entertainment or hospitality fields. He earns money from the sale of property, vehicles and home articles.

Famous people with this yoga

Jean-Paul Belmondo, actor; Dirk Bogarde, actor; David Cassidy, singer/actor; Anton Chekhov, writer; Johnny Dundee, boxer; King Farouk, Egyptian royalty; Helen Frankenthaler, artist; Frederic Van Norstrand, astrologer.

Case study

King Farouk, the last king of Egypt, was educated in England and ruled 1937-1952. His reign began with promise but ended in scandal. Farouk loved a glamorous lifestyle. Although owning vast properties, dozens of palaces and hundreds of cars, he often went to Europe for shopping sprees.

His interests leaned away from politics and toward fast cars and women. His personal vehicle was a red 1947 Bentley. Married three times, he had dozens of mistresses.

His appetite was legendary. Breakfast was 30 eggs with toast and sweet tea. After a dinner of lobster, steak or lamb, he'd snack on caviar or ice cream. It's said that he ate 600 oysters a week. Although he never drank alcohol, the slender boy-king became a bloated gourmand who couldn't get into his sports car.

He had a lifelong habit of collecting. He owned a 94-carat diamond and other jewels. He amassed one of the world's finest coin collections, and was reputed to own a huge collection of pornography.

With Farouk regarded a corrupt playboy, an army coup in 1952 forced his abdication. Exiled in Rome, he indulged himself in every debauchery, growing increasingly obese, "a stomach with a head." He rented entire hotels for parties and gambled with pathological abandon in Monte Carlo. At restaurants he'd literally order everything on the menu. While stuffing himself one night, a heart attack killed him at age 45.

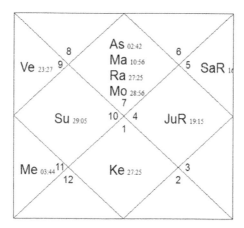

The Sun in 4th house Capricorn exchanges with Saturn in 11th house Leo. Saturn is strong because retrograde. Pre-exchange, the Sun is involved in no other yoga, while Saturn's opposition to Mercury creates a *Dharma Karma Adhipati Yoga*.

Both pre- and post-exchange, Saturn aspects the ascendant, the 10th lord Moon and 2nd lord Mars, thus ruining his reputation through his dissolute lifestyle, and his health through bad diet.

4th house themes are evident in the initial embrace of his people (as the first Arab-speaking Egyptian king), and his great love of cars. 11th house themes played out in his over-the-top social life, and his unchecked desire to collect almost everything he coveted.

(Note: in *Light on Life*, deFouw & Svoboda, the common significations of the 11th house include jewelry, vehicles, the paraphernalia of luxury, and playful sexual acts.)

Whereas the Sun is ordinary, Saturn is retrograde, and therefore qualifies as the control planet for this exchange. Its placement in the 11th house is but a sad reflection of Farouk's playboy lifestyle, since he accomplished nothing of political consequence in his 15-year reign except to indulge himself in luxuries and parties.

Exchange of 4th and 12th lords

Parashara says:

- *If the 4th lord is situated in the 12th house, the native will be devoid of domestic and other comforts, will have vices and be foolish and indolent.* (BPHS 26:48)

- *In the event of the 12th lord being placed in the 4th house, the native will be devoid of maternal happiness and will day by day have losses in respect of lands, conveyances and houses.* (BPHS 26:136)

This is a *Dainya Parivartana Yoga* wherein the lords are in a mutual 5/9 relationship from *moksha* houses. Because of this relationship, the native may appear restless, seeking release from the confines of home, maternal influence, community values or conventional morality.

The native needs lengthy periods of quiet and tranquility to find peace within his heart. For this reason, he takes retreats in ashrams or places of worship. Since his happiness depends upon his spiritual liberation, he may surrender his attachments to property in order to be free. He lives a vagrant life for periods of time, and is an advocate of the homeless.

He is prone to illness and his health gradually suffers. His mother suffers poor health as well, and her longevity is poor. Nevertheless, she too undertakes foreign travels.

His happiness depends upon his sexual fulfillment, and he experiences a struggle between his spiritual aspirations and sexual desires. He has sexual relations with a woman who is similar in appearance or temperament to his mother.

Foreign travel is a major life theme. He travels in search of spiritual liberation, and makes his residence abroad. He pursues his education in a foreign country. He buys foreign property, suffers losses through property investments, or gives up a portion of his property to another. He owns or leases a foreign car.

Because he is philosophically unattached, he becomes involved in charities and not-for-profit organizations, especially those with an international scope of operations.

Famous people with this yoga

Roseanne Barr, comedienne; Roberto Benigni, actor; William Burroughs, writer; Kirk Douglas, actor; Sandy Duncan, actress; John Ehrlichman, Presidential advisor; Melissa Etheridge, musician; Richard Houck, astrologer; Janis Joplin, singer; Ken Keyes, archetypal hippy; Thomas Merton, writer/mystic; Louis XV, King of France; Liz Smith, gossip columnist; Simon Wiesenthal, Nazi hunter.

Case study

Thomas Merton was a French-American writer, poet, monk, mystic and social critic whose writing reached the bestseller lists. In 1941 he entered a Trappist monastery in rural Kentucky and was ordained in 1949 after eight years of silence.

He was a study in contradictions. He craved solitude, but also enjoyed the occasional drink, loved jazz, and delighted in scatological humor. He rose daily at 3:15 AM to pray for seven hours, but once fell recklessly in love with a woman half his age.

An expert Latinist, he translated all the works of the 13th-century monastic masters. His first book, *Seven Storey Mountain* sold 600,000 copies in its first year, capturing readers like few books since Saint Augustine's *Confessions*. A prolific writer, he wrote more than 70 books, mostly on spirituality, social justice and pacifism.

His death was bizarre. During a six-month trip through Asia, the longest of his otherwise cloistered life, he stepped out of a shower in a cottage near Bangkok, reached for a fan with defective wiring and was instantly electrocuted.

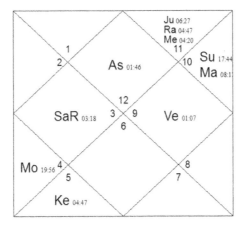

Saturn in 4th house Gemini exchanges with Mercury in 12th house Aquarius. Saturn is strong because retrograde. Mercury is associated with *lagnesh* Jupiter, a combination that creates two *Dharma Karma Adhipati Yogas*. This pairing of two intellectual planets in the 12th is further amplified by their close alignment with Rahu.

Pre- or post-exchange, Jupiter influences both the 4th and 12th houses and their lords, thus reinforcing the pursuit of *moksha* via a cloistered life, and the sharing of wisdom through his prolific spiritual writings.

The 4th/12th exchange played itself out in multiple ways: many changes of residence throughout his childhood, time spent at French boarding schools, university education in England and, ultimately, immigration to America. On a more personal level, his mother died of stomach cancer when he was only seven.

During his university years at Cambridge, 12th house themes emerged via a relatively dissolute lifestyle – reckless spending, nights spent drinking in jazz clubs, and womanizing.

In his maturity, the 12th house revealed the other side of its coin in seclusion, monastic life, vows of renunciation and meditation. He also became a keen proponent of inter-faith understanding, especially Eastern religions, and engaged in dialogue and correspondence with leading figures like the Dalai Lama, DT Suzuki and Thich Nhat Hanh.

Ultimately, death in a foreign land is also a 4th/12th signature.

Although Mercury is normal and Saturn is retrograde, we might in this case question Saturn's eligibility to assume control of this exchange. Mercury forms two *Raja Yogas* with *lagnesh* Jupiter and receives further karmic thrust from Rahu, which is very much at home in Aquarius. Thus, Mercury's placement in the 12th becomes the more appropriate signature of a monastic life.

EXCHANGES INVOLVING THE 5TH HOUSE LORD

Exchange of 5th and 6th lords

Parashara says:

- *In the event of the 5th lord being relegated to the 6th house, the native's son will be equal to his enemy, or he will die, or the native will acquire an adopted or a purchased son.* (BPHS 26:54)

- *In the event of the 6th lord occupying the 5th house, the native's wealth will be always fluctuating, he will contract enmity with his son and friend, be happy, selfish and kind.* (BPHS 26:65)

This is a *Dainya Parivartana Yoga* wherein the lords are in a mutual 2/12 relationship. This dynamic may cause problems with the cognitive faculties, spiritual practices and children.

The native lacks mental clarity and experiences intellectual obstacles that affect his studies. His spiritual practices are inconsistent, based upon competition and the desire to gain something over others, ie, spiritual materialism. He develops a sort of religious fanaticism and is intolerant of other faiths.

He has health problems, the sources of which are mental or spiritual. Hypochondria is one possible manifestation, spiritual malaise another. The weak link is often the digestive system.

In romance, he invites conflicts. He tries to gain intimacy too quickly, and treats the partner with hostility if things don't go his way. He acts in an unscrupulous and self-serving manner, and may cheat on his partner.

The person can experience problems having children, eg, abortions, miscarriages or premature illnesses terminating the child's life. Even if the person has a child, there is friction between them, such that real enmity may develop. If lieu of having a child naturally, adoption is a possibility. Children are a cause of worry on account of their health, although they enjoy financial success.

He is employed in a field related to education, the entertainment industry or creative endeavors of some sort. His investments may not pan out. He acts upon a self-defeating intuition, and sustains losses despite repeated attempts to profit. His enemies are numerous, and they interfere with his luck in life.

Famous people with this yoga

Susan Atkins, cult killer; Bjorn Borg, tennis player; E.E. Cummings, poet; Otto Hahn, scientist; Jeddu Krishnamurti, guru; Elisabeth Kubler-Ross, psychiatrist; Alphee Lavoie, astrologer; Gordon Lightfoot, musician; Jackie Mason, comedian; Matthew McConaughey, actor; John Milton, poet; Michael Munkasey, astrologer; Kenny Rogers, entertainer; Murray Rose, Olympic swimmer; David Souter, Supreme Court jurist; William Styron, writer; Jerry West, basketball player.

Case study

Elisabeth Kubler-Ross was a Swiss psychiatrist and author who became famous for her book, *On Death and Dying*, chronicling her work with terminal patients. Educated first as a doctor, against the objections of her father, she later became very critical of the medical profession.

She was an ardent hiker, mountain climber and skier. She admitted to a short fuse, great highs and lows and an overly idealistic nature. She had an excellent memory, nearly total recall, and was a workaholic.

She had several out-of-the-body experiences during her lifetime, was interested in the occult, and through her counseling of the terminally ill, became expert in the five stages of grief: denial, anger, bargaining, depression, and acceptance.

She was the recipient of 20 honorary degrees and taught over 125,000 students in death and dying courses at colleges, seminaries, medical schools, hospitals, and social-work institutions.

One of her ambitions was to build a hospice for children with AIDS. But when she announced in Virginia that she was adopting 20 HIV-infected babies, her house was burned to the ground and her pet llama was shot.

Despite four miscarriages, she had one son and one daughter. She suffered a series of strokes that left her confined to a wheelchair until her death.

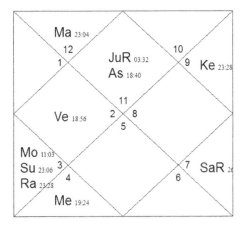

The Moon in 5th house Gemini exchanges with Mercury in 6th house Cancer. The Moon is weak, being in the last *tithi* before the new moon. Mercury is ordinary but aspected by a powerful (exalted and retrograde) Saturn.

The themes of the 5th/6th exchange were revealed in personal health difficulties, including a near-death experience due to a bowel obstruction. Four out of six pregnancies resulted in miscarriages.

The 5th/6th exchange also reflected her compassion for the sick, especially children, as evidenced in her work with HIV-infected infants, which ambition brought her into conflict with her local community. Even her pet became collateral damage in this battle (the 6th represents pets, and the 5th is their loss).

No stranger to 6th house conflict, she was known as being abrasive and critical of the medical profession. She was nonetheless acknowledged as a compassionate caregiver, providing assistance in their dying moments to over 20,000 terminal patients.

The Moon is weak because it is dark and waning within one *tithi* of the Sun, while Mercury is simply ordinary. As such, it can be considered the control planet for this exchange. Its placement in the 6th house is entirely consistent with her role as caregiver to the terminally ill. Note also that the 6th is the 12th (surrender) for the other.

Exchange of 5th and 7th lords

Parashara says:

- *If the 5th lord is situated in the 7th house, the native will be tolerant of all religions and very religious, endowed with progenic happiness, and be helpful to others.* (BPHS 26:55)

- *Should the 7th lord occupy the 5th house, the native will be a man of honor, gifted with all the virtues, always delighted, and endowed with all kinds of wealth.* (BPHS 26:77)

This is a *Maha Parivartana Yoga* (also a *Dharma Karma Adhipati Yoga*) with the lords in a mutual 3/11 relationship. Because of this pattern, there's mental preoccupation with relationships of all kinds, whether social, professional or intimate.

The native is spiritually inclined, travels to seek enlightenment, and is tolerant of other faiths. He is clever in business, and succeeds in fields of speculation, sports, entertainment, and anything to do with children. He is a good deal-maker, and is skilled in forging contracts and agreements.

He has an active intellect, often has sex on his mind, and is very attracted to ephemeral relationships. He develops a love affair during the course of his education. He finds (monogamous) marital life a strain, and is frequently separated from his spouse and children.

His spouse is active, intelligent, spiritual and youthful. The spouse succeeds through her own efforts, but her longevity is not good. His children are adventurous, athletic, artistic, interested in travel and productive in earning a good income.

This exchange favors careers in political diplomacy, talent representation, and creative collaboration of all sorts.

Famous people with this yoga

Warren Beatty, actor; Hector Berlioz, composer; Judy Blume, writer; Roger Corman, director; Christopher Darden, attorney; Daniel Day-Lewis, actor; Richard Idemon, astrologer; Lindsay Lohan, actor; Bette Bao Lord, writer; Anne McCaffrey, writer; James Earl Ray, assassin; Curtis Sliwa, Guardian Angel; Marcia Starck, astrologer; Duke of Wellington, militarist; Malcolm X, political activist.

Case study

Warren Beatty is an American actor, producer, screenwriter and director. Strikingly handsome with a style that is self-consciously cool and opaque, he was the classic screen idol of his day. He has been nominated for 14 Oscars, including his performance in 1967 for *Bonnie and Clyde*. He won the Oscar as Best Director in 1981 for *Reds*.

Although known more for his acting than his writing, Beatty was nominated four times for Best Screenplay, which he received three times. He is the only person to have been nominated for best producer, director, writer and actor in the same film, both for *Heaven Can Wait* and *Reds*.

Aside from his movie career, Beatty has achieved the dubious reputation of having been a notorious womanizer and lover to a large number of Hollywood and society women. A partial list includes Cher, Brigitte Bardot, Elle Macpherson, Goldie Hawn, Jackie Onassis, Joan Collins, Joni Mitchell, Madonna and Mary Tyler Moore.

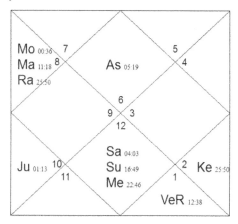

Jupiter in 5th house Capricorn exchanges with Saturn in 7th house Pisces. Jupiter is debilitated and forms no other yoga. Saturn is associated with *lagnesh* Mercury to form two *Dharma Karma Adhipati Yogas*.

The 5th/7th exchange played out in an extremely active sex life, wherein this notion of sex-on-the-brain (5th house mind, 7th house sex) is pretty much epitomized in Warren Beatty's pre-marital lifestyle.

The same exchange can also be used to explain his highly creative role in the course of his movie career, whether as a writer involved in multiple projects (many of which fell by the wayside), as a director marshaling creative talent, or more generically, in his sometimes-spotty record as producer in collaboration with many of Hollywood's luminaries of the day, in front of or behind the camera.

Jupiter is debilitated but Saturn has *dig bala*, thus qualifying it as the control planet for this exchange. Certainly its placement in the 7th house highlights his infamous love life prior to marriage.

Exchange of 5th and 8th lords

Parashara says:

- *In the event of the 5th lord being relegated to the 8th house, the native will have less progenic happiness, will be troubled by cough and pulmonary or respiratory diseases, be given to anger and be devoid of happiness.* (BPHS 26:56)

- *If the 8th lord happens to fall in the 5th house, the native will be dull witted. He will have a few children and be long-lived and wealthy.* (BPHS 26:89)

This is a *Dainya Parivartana Yoga* wherein the lords are in a mutual 4/10 relationship. Because of this dynamic, mental stress and trauma arises.

The native's *purva punya* (karma from the previous life) renders a dulled intellect, such that his mind occupies a *tamasik* state, incapable of contemplating a higher order of things. As a result of flawed thinking, he commits sins, first through his thoughts, then through actions that lead to his self-undoing.

His mind is often concerned, even obsessed, with sexual subjects. He may have an unusual, even aberrant, sexuality. He may have suffered sexual abuse as a child. He suffers psychosomatic ills, wherein the mind itself is the primary cause of feeling ill-at-ease. Anger is a root cause of many ills.

His love affairs are generally unhappy, falling into a sort of love/hate relationship, where an all-or-nothing attitude prevails.

He experiences difficulties with respect to children, eg, abortion, miscarriage, illness, accidents. Even if his children are healthy, there are problems in their lives, or in his relationship with them. In extreme cases, there may be death of children. He receives no benefits through inheritance, although his children do. His children may be involved in the purchase and sale of vehicles or properties.

He is interested in esoteric or occult subjects. Mysteries, death, and the after-life are fascinations for him. He may study subjects so far removed from the contemporary that they seem "dead", eg, the so-called dead languages, archaeology, antiques, occult subjects, etc.

He makes bad investments, suffers irrevocable losses, and goes into debt. Gambling may become an obsession.

Famous people with this yoga

Johann Elert Bode, astronomer; Honoré Daumier, artist; Roy Firebrace, astrologer; Amy Fisher, attempted murderer; Jean Harlow, actress; Lena Horne, singer; Johannes Kepler, astronomer; Sam Peckinpah, director; Harold Pinter, playwright; Jane Roberts, mystic/author; Dennis Rodman, basketball player; Diana Ross, singer; Ian Douglas Smith, politician; Jackie Stewart, race car driver.

Case study

Dennis Rodman is a retired American professional basketball forward, who played for the Detroit Pistons, Chicago Bulls and other NBA teams. He has also been a professional wrestler and an actor in several reality series. His visibility as a professional athlete was further leveraged by his exhibitionistic attire and personal adornment, including wearing articles of women's clothing on the basketball court.

Rodman experienced an unhappy childhood, thinks about death a lot and has seriously contemplated suicide at least once. Post-NBA, his career has lurched from one misadventure to another, including celebrity wrestling matches and reality shows. Substance abuse continues to dog him, and he's gotten into trouble numerous times, mouthing obscenities or saying outrageous things while on camera.

Aside from a relationship with Madonna and a very short marriage to Carmen Electra, his best friend has been Kim Jong Un, the boy-dictator of North Korea. Rodman's relationship with Kim Jong Un has baffled his fans and the US State Department alike.

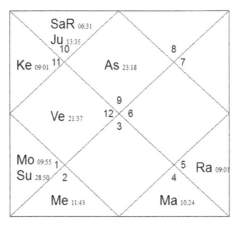

The Moon in 5th house Aries exchanges with Mars in 8th house Cancer. Both are weak – the Moon within two *tithis* of a new moon, Mars debilitated. However, Mars is in mutual aspect with debilitated *lagnesh* Jupiter, a combination that produces two *Dharma Karma Adhipati Yogas*. Mars also mutually aspects a very powerful Saturn (retrograde and in its own sign) which creates a *Dhana Yoga*.

The 5th house themes are revealed in his gamesmanship, showmanship, eclectic love life that included a transsexual partner, and his declaration that he thinks like a bisexual. The 8th house of irregularities reveals itself in various peculiarities, whether in his choice of attire, friendships or career pursuits.

The archetypal party animal, he's had many altercations with the police, including drunk driving, domestic abuse and no less than 70 calls for police to quell loud noise from his raucous house parties.

The Moon is weak because it's dark and waning, while Mars is debilitated, thus obliging us to consider the lesser of two evils. Despite its debility, Mars forms several yogas (two with *lagnesh* Jupiter) while the Moon forms none. Thus, Mars becomes the control planet for this exchange. Its placement in the 8th house is representative of Rodman's public role as rebellious oddball.

Exchange of 5th and 9th lords

Parashara says:

- *Should the 5th lord be placed in the 9th house, the native will be a prince or equal to a prince, be an illustrious author, and be illustrious in his family.* (BPHS 26:57)

- *Should the 9th lord be placed in the 5th house, the native will have the blessings of sons and good fortune. He will be devoted to his elders and teachers, will have fortitude, be religious and charitable and learned.* (BPHS 26:101)

This is a *Maha Parivartana Yoga* (also a *Raja Yoga*) wherein the lords are in a mutual 5/9 relationship from *trikona* houses. Because of this dynamic, the mind operates at a sublime level.

The native is healthy, wealthy and prosperous. He benefits from *purva punya* (good karma from his past life), and applies it via positive actions, *kriyamana karma*, in the current lifetime. He has strong spiritual beliefs, and is a devout practitioner of his religion. He may be initiated into the use of mantras or some other spiritual practice by a guru of a high order.

Both his father and his children are fortunate, well-educated, morally upright and successful. His father pursues higher studies in combination with foreign travel. His children gain through speculation, games of chance or creative pursuits.

He views his romantic relationships in a spiritual context. He places less emphasis on the material or sexual benefits of a relationship, and more on the karmic "correctness" of such a relationship as a vehicle for spiritual growth. He encounters romantic partners on distant journeys, on spiritual quests, or in academic surroundings.

His mind is naturally drawn to higher studies, and he is inclined to pursue an intellectual profession in communication or education. He is interested in writing and philosophy, and may author books on spiritual subjects or related travels.

Famous people with this yoga

Jim Clark, race car driver; Quentin Crisp, humorist; Simone de Beauvoir, writer; Emperor Hirohito, Japanese royalty; Jeff Jawer, astrologer; Tad Mann, astrologer; Lyle Menendez, patricide/matricide; Richard Speck, mass murderer; James Woods, actor; Gian-Franco Zeffirelli, director.

Case study

Simone de Beauvoir was a French writer and existentialist teacher who enjoyed a literary career as a novelist, philosopher, essayist and memoirist. A political activist rather than a feminist, she had an unconventional morality that rejected marriage for women in favor of autonomy.

She was deeply religious as a child, at one point intending to become a nun, but had a crisis of faith at age 14, after which she became an atheist. She was academically accomplished, gaining degrees in both math and philosophy before teaching at the Sorbonne.

A major participant in the Existentialist movement, along with Jean Paul Sartre, her life companion in an open relationship, she wrote books that examined the position of women in a male-dominated world. She traveled extensively and wrote popular travel diaries about time spent in the United States and China.

She had a number of female lovers, some of whom she shared with Sartre. The nature of these relationships, some of which began while she was a professor, later led to her suspension from teaching at the Sorbonne.

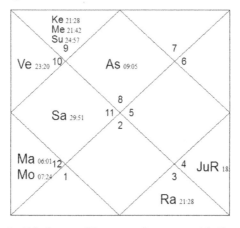

The Moon in 5th house Pisces exchanges with Jupiter in 9th house Cancer. The two are natural benefics and *sattvik* planets. The Moon is associated with *lagnesh* Mars, which creates both a *Chandra Mangala* Yoga and a *Dharma Karma Adhipati Yoga*.

Jupiter is very strong, being both retrograde and exalted, and from the 9th enjoys a mutual aspect with Venus, thus creating a *Dharma Karma Adhipati Yoga*.

Whether pre- or post-exchange, Jupiter bestows its influence on all three of the *lagna*, *lagnesh* Mars and the Moon, thus bolstering her reputation as an archetypal woman of the modern era. Furthermore, with all three *dharma* lords remaining in *dharma* houses, her "canonization" as a feminist role model was more or less assured.

The 5th house themes are revealed through her prodigious intellect, eg, degrees in both math and philosophy and in her authorship of several books, both fiction and non-fiction, which garnered literary awards and popular acclaim.

The 9th house themes were revealed through academia (she taught at the Sorbonne for 12 years), her publishing career and her increasing profile as an existential theorist for women's liberation and the feminist movement.

The Moon is ordinary while Jupiter is both exalted and retrograde, thus clinching its role as control planet for this exchange. Its position in the 9th house is a classic signature for an academic and philosopher.

Exchange of 5th and 10th lords

Parashara says:

- *Should the 5th lord occupy the 10th house, the native will be blessed with Raj yoga (governmental favor), and various pleasures and be very illustrious.* (BPHS 26:58)

- *In the event of the 10th lord being placed in the 5th house, the native will be endowed with all kinds of learning, be always cheerful, wealthy and be blessed with sons.* (BPHS 26:113)

This is a *Maha Parivartana Yoga* (also a *Dharma Karma Adhipati Yoga*) wherein the lords are in a mutual 6/8 relationship. Because of this pattern, we get a sense of the mind really being "put to work" in the name of professional pursuits.

The native enjoys a high degree of luck in his career and is fortunate in achieving his aspirations for success, reputation and social status. He has an intellectual profession, and succeeds in government, law, general management, public administration and the investment industry.

His children are successful in their careers, but are prone to getting into situations of debt and/or litigation. They are also a source of worry on account of their health.

His intellectual skills are somehow put on public display, eg, through an artistic profession such as author, actor or other public performer. His writing skills are often applied to corporate purposes: public relations, speechwriting, annual reports, business plans, and legal contracts.

He may exercise a flair for dramatics or showmanship in some aspect of a public career. This could favor professions as diverse as politician, news anchor, motivational speaker or sports commentator.

Famous people with this yoga

Kareem Abdul-Jabbar, basketball player; Charles E.O. Carter, astrologer; Hillary Clinton, politician; André Courreges, designer; Jeff Green, astrologer; Sybil Leek, astrologer; Robert Mapplethorpe, photographer; Marcel Marceau, mime; Josef Mengele, Nazi doctor; Vaslav Nijinski, ballet dancer; Philip Roth, writer; Zucchero, singer.

Case study

Hillary Clinton is an American attorney, politician and prominent member of the Democrat party. From the time she was president of her high school class, she brought home academic honors. Socially conscious, she was always a shrewd and capable organizer, a graduate of Yale Law School.

Over the years she's been First Lady to President Bill Clinton, the first female Senator elected to represent the State of New York, and the US Secretary of State under the Obama administration. As Secretary of State, she visited more countries than any other predecessor.

The National Law Journal has twice listed her as one of the 100 most influential lawyers in America. She's the only First Lady to have been subpoenaed (for the Whitewater investigation), and the only First Lady to have ever run for office. Over the course of Bill Clinton's role as Governor of Arkansas and President of the USA, she has endured both the Gennifer Flowers and Monica Lewinsky scandals, maintaining a stoic public persona despite privately engaging in loud fights with her errant husband.

She has authored five books and become a shining example, both of grace under pressure and what a woman can accomplish in public service. As of April 2015, she has announced her candidacy for the 2016 Presidential elections.

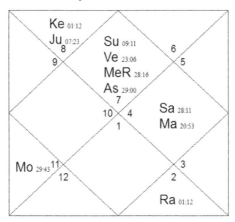

The Moon in 5th house Aquarius exchanges with Saturn in 10th house Cancer. Pre-exchange, Saturn forms both a *Dharma Karma Adhipati Yoga* and a *Dhana Yoga* with a mixed-condition Mars (*dig bala* but *neecha*).

Pre- or post-exchange, that debilitated Mars influences both the 5th and 10th houses and their lords, thus provoking both grudging admiration for Clinton's intelligence and resistance to her confrontational positions.

The 5th house themes are revealed in her populist appeal, her authorship, and her devotion to her daughter Chelsea. The 5th also represents ministerial roles, which she has fulfilled in one capacity or another throughout her career.

The 10th house themes play out in her various government positions, her high socio-political profile and her strong advocacy of Democrat principles both at home and abroad. The presence of that mixed-condition Mars, troubling whichever of the exchange planets share the 10th with it, might in part explain the scandals that have dogged her public life.

Government involvement itself is a combined influence of 5th (ministerial), 9th (legislative) and 10th (public) house roles, and this yoga invokes two of them.

The Moon and Saturn are both ordinary, so there is no obvious control planet for this exchange. That leaves us with coequal houses – the 5th for governmental ministry, the 10th for her social status. If push came to shove, we could favor Saturn because it forms two yogas with Mars, even though it might only highlight her checkered reputation.

Exchange of 5th and 11th lords

Parashara says:

- *In case the 5th lord occupies the 11th house, the native will be learned, be dear to the people, be an illustrious author, be very skillful, and be endowed with many sons and wealth.* (BPHS 26:59)

- *If the 11th lord is placed in the 5th house, the native's children will be happy, educated and virtuous. He himself will be religious and happy.* (BPHS 26:125)

This is a *Maha Parivartana Yoga* (also a *Dhana Yoga*) wherein the lords are in a mutual 7/7 relationship. Note that the *sambandha* between these two lords in mutual aspect further strengthens each other's significations.

The native is an eternal optimist, indulging in anticipation of dreams to be fulfilled. He is preoccupied with earning money. He pursues an education in a related field, such as commerce or finance, and uses his knowledge for further profit.

His children earn wealth in the entertainment or sports fields, although their life spans may be shorter than average. They are fond of travel.

His friends or elder siblings are intellectual, creative and spiritual. They help the native by offering advice on investments, or making introductions within their network. The elder sibling is likely to have a short life span.

The native gains from lotteries, gambling, horse races, and stock market speculation. He may work as an investment advisor, stockbroker, bookie, or casino operator. His considerable writing skills may be applied to the fields of commerce and entertainment, organizational and community activities, or politics.

Famous people with this yoga

Enrico Caruso, opera singer; Marc Garneau, astronaut; Victor Hugo, writer; Edna O'Brien, writer; Maritha Pottenger, astrologer; Rudolph Steiner, philosopher; Cat Stevens, musician; Douglas Wilder, politician; Vladimir Zhirinovsky, politician.

Case study

Victor Hugo was a French writer, poet, dramatist, novelist, essayist, painter, architect and critic – an eclectic genius who was also a politically active humanitarian. His most famous works include *The Hunchback of Notre Dame* and *Les Miserables*.

He wrote his first play at age 14. After a period of extreme poverty, he was awarded an annual pension by Louis XVIII. He went on to become the most prolific French writer of the 19th century, writing 100 lines of verse or 20 pages of prose each day, many of his works criticizing social and political injustices of the day.

Hugo was elected to the French Academy and became a member of the National Assembly. In his 81st year, the street of his residence was renamed Avenue Victor Hugo.

He was married but also had mistresses throughout his life. Out of his four children, one daughter went insane and another drowned. A lusty man, he recorded his many sexual encounters up until seven weeks before his death.

He was one of the most famous men in the world at that time and was a millionaire when he died. The day of his funeral, crowds were so vast that 10,000 police were needed to hold them back. Drunken bodies littered the Champs-Elysées. Even the brothels were closed.

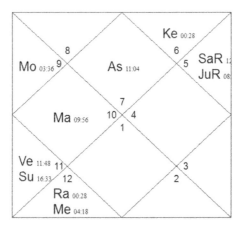

The Sun in 5th house Aquarius exchanges with Saturn in 11th house Leo. These two malefics are mutual enemies but, while occupying each other's sign, aspect their own. The Sun is ordinary while Saturn is strong through retrogression.

Whether before or after exchange, the Sun and Saturn both continue to be in association or mutual aspect with *lagnesh* Venus, which generates a *Dhana Yoga* through the Sun, and two *Dharma-Karma Adhipati Yogas* through Saturn. Independently, the Sun in mutual aspect with Saturn generates another *Dhana Yoga*.

The 5th house themes are exemplified by his enormous creative output, his amorous nature throughout life and the tragic deaths of two daughters, one of which permanently scarred him.

The 11th house themes played out via his active involvement in social causes of the day, including his leadership of a literary rebellion called the Romantic Movement, his participation in the National Assembly, and his later appointment as a senator.

The Sun is ordinary while Saturn is retrograde, thus making it the control planet for this exchange. Its occupation of the 11th house invokes the essential humanitarianism for which Hugo was much loved.

Exchange of 5th and 12th lords

Parashara says:

- *In the event of the 5th lord having fallen in the 12th house, the native is bereft of the happiness of having his own sons. He will have an adopted or purchased son.* (BPHS 26:60)

- *Should the 12th lord occupy the 5th house, the native will be bereft of sons and learning. He will spend money and also make pilgrimages to beget a son.* (BPHS 26:137)

This is a *Dainya Parivartana Yoga* wherein the lords are in a mutual 6/8 relationship. Because of this dynamic, the native experiences delusions.

The native is naturally introspective, but with a tendency to daydream, so he may have difficulty functioning in the real world. He lacks peace of mind, and has a troubled dream life. His logic is faulty. He is deceptive, or experiences confusion in dealing with others.

He dreams of liberation, or *moksha*, but lacks the mental discipline to pursue a spiritual path. Mantra, meditation and other spiritual practices don't come easily to him.

He thinks a lot about sex but is sexually ambivalent. Therefore, he experiences unconscious desires for partners who are unsuited by virtue of disposition, gender, availability, etc. He may fear real intimacy, and end up forming relationships with people at a distance so as to avoid regular close contact. Attraction to foreigners is a typical occurrence.

There are barriers to progeny. The person may be afraid to have children, but even when the desire is there, there are delays, miscarriages or outright denial. As an alternative, the person may adopt. There are worries on account of children, and poor rapport between them. Even if the relationship is sound, such a person's children find it difficult to become settled in life.

He has problems with his investments and is more likely to generate losses than profits. As a consequence, he worries a lot. He has no particular aptitude for sports, and has a fear of public performance.

Famous people with this yoga

Lynn Anderson, singer; Stephen Arroyo, astrologer; Fred Astaire, dancer; Pieter Botha, politician; L. Ron Hubbard, Scientologist; Annie Lennox, singer; Dick Martin, comedian; Alfred de Musset, playwright; Pablo Picasso, artist; Susan St. James, actress.

Case study

Pablo Picasso was a Spanish artist who lived most of his life in France. He's considered to be the most original and influential visual artist of the early 20th century. His Herculean output, estimated at 50,000 individual works of art, made him a billionaire at his death.

The eldest of three children, Pablo is said to have been born dead, "awakened" when a visitor blew cigar smoke in his face and made him cry. As a child, he was surrounded by females, learned macho behavior early, and ultimately became a first-class manipulator of women.

He was a child prodigy and once said, "I never drew like a child. When I was 12, I drew like Raphael." He discovered bohemian life in his late teens, and was rumored to have had a homosexual relationship with a gypsy boy at age 17.

At age 20, Picasso set up a studio in Paris and began signing his work with his mother's maiden name. Living in total poverty, he worked far into the night, producing museum quality paintings.

With a roving eye and sexual appetite bordering on gluttony, he married twice and engaged in multiple affairs. Beauty and relative youth were the only consistent qualities he desired in women. In his 60s his sexual gluttony became obsessive.

~

Mercury in 5th house Scorpio exchanges with Mars in 12th house Gemini. Mercury, an enemy of Mars, is associated with the dark and debilitated *lagnesh* Moon, and aligned with the Rahu-Ketu axis. Mercury forms no productive yoga, neither with the Moon nor Jupiter. Mars is isolated in the 12th, aspected only by a debilitated Saturn.

Whether pre- or post-exchange, Mars influences (along with Saturn) the 12th house of bed pleasures, thus invoking an image of a satyr at work and play.

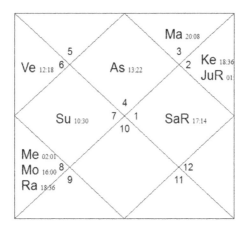

The 5th house themes were reflected in his staggering artistic output, his cavalier attitude towards both lovers and children, and his stomach ulcers.

The 12th house themes played out primarily in sexual obsession, to such a degree that it pervaded his art, wherein several works feature an aged dwarf-like artist ravishing his beautiful young models.

The extraordinary aspect of Picasso's chart is that he had four debilitated planets and very few yogas. Aside from the Moon forming *Raja Yoga* with Rahu, and a *Dharma-Karma Adhipati Yoga* with Jupiter, the 5th/12th *Parivartana Yoga* is perhaps the one combination that epitomized his life.

Mercury and Mars are both ordinary, tainted by the influence of a debilitated planet, and form no other yoga. Therefore, we might say there is no control planet for this exchange. Thus, we're left with a coequal influence of two houses – the 5th for Picasso's enormous creativity, and the 12th for the sexuality that pervaded both his lifestyle and art.

Exchanges Involving the 6th House Lord

Exchange of 6th and 7th lords

Parashara says:

- *In case the 6th lord is situated in the 7th house, the native will be devoid of happiness through wedlock, be famous, virtuous, honorable, adventurous and wealthy.* (BPHS 26:67)

- *If the 7th lord is placed in the 6th house, the native's wife will be sickly or the native is inimical towards her, he is himself given to anger and remains devoid of happiness.* (BPHS 26:78)

This is a *Dainya Parivartana Yoga* wherein the lords are in a mutual 2/12 relationship. Because of this dynamic, the yoga typically plays out in flawed relationships.

The native experiences much open opposition, in the form of competitors or enemies who create trouble in his life. Professionally, this suggests a career related to defense, police, or security work. Alternatively, he may work as a lawyer, mediator, or paralegal in the justice system.

He experiences fluctuations in the state of his health, particularly the kidneys. He has problems with his sexual organs, externally via injury or rash, or internally via deformation. His sexual performance is affected, such that he is physically exhausted through too much sex, or incapable of performing.

His spouse is passionate and adversarial. Marriage is a constant strain, with regular conflict on an emotional, verbal and perhaps physical level. In due course, separation may be the ultimate outcome. Alternatively, the spouse may be unhealthy, with frequent illnesses and complaints, both real and imagined. The spouse makes poor investments, or is taken advantage of in some way, such that their finances suffer.

The native or his spouse may work as a vet or animal caregiver, but as likely as not, one of them will simply feel a very strong attachment to pets, such that the animal becomes almost as important as the spouse.

Famous people with this yoga

Les Aspin, politician; Berndt Andreas Baader, anarchist; Robert A. Bloch, writer; Pat Boone, singer; Jack Bruce, musician; James Caan, actor; Nick Campion, astrologer; Dennis Hopper, actor; Kitaro, musician; Jean Monnet, economist; Czar Nicholas II, Russian royalty; Tom Paxton, folksinger; Dane Rudhyar, astrologer; David Sanborn, musician; Terrence Stamp, actor; Natalie Wood, actress.

Case study

Dane Rudhyar was a French-American astrologer, one of the most notable and respected of the 20th century. He was the pioneer of modern transpersonal astrology, his best known work being *The Astrology of Personality*.

He was called a modern Renaissance man for his ability to express himself in music, painting, poetry, philosophy and metaphysics. He wrote for national magazines since the 1930s and was the author of many books – astrology, fiction, poetry and metaphysics.

Rudhyar had poor health as a child and at age 12 had a kidney removed. He majored in philosophy and graduated from the Sorbonne at age 16. While involved in the artistic and musical climate of Paris, he had a mystical experience in which he became aware of the cyclic nature of all human existence, from which time on he sought to gain a deeper understanding through the study of theosophy, Eastern religions, Jungian psychology and astrology.

He immigrated to the USA and spent his final years in San Francisco where he became a central figure in the New Age movement of the 60s. His appreciation for intelligent women resulted in his being married five times.

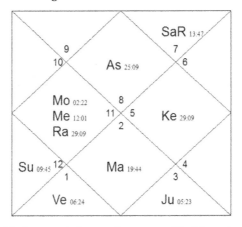

Venus in 6th house Aries exchanges with Mars in 7th house Taurus. Pre-exchange, neither forms yoga with any other planet. Before or after exchange, one or the other is afflicted by a powerful (exalted and retrograde) Saturn.

A 6th/7th exchange is almost a kiss of death for relationships, spelling problems for the couple, or the partner. (Since the 7th indicates relationships, the 6th is the 12th from the 7th and therefore the undoing of a relationship.) The aspect of a powerful Saturn on Venus, which is both 7th lord and *karaka* for relationships, makes this pattern all the more potent.

This loss-of-relationship presaged by the 6th/7th exchange was seen in Rudhyar's being married five times. Interestingly enough, the same exchange also explains his loss of a kidney, since the 7th house rules the kidneys.

Both Mars and Venus are ordinary and form no yogas, so determining a control planet for this exchange is a tough call. Since Mars is *lagnesh*, we might favor it. A natural agitator, its placement in the 7th house evokes his turbulent marital life.

Exchange of 6th and 8th lords

Parashara says:

- *In the event of the 6th lord falling in the 8th house, the native will be sickly, inimical to the learned and the wise, will desire others' wealth, be interested in others' wives, and be impure.* (BPHS 26:68)

- *In case the 8th lord is gone in the 6th house, the native will win over his opponents, will have a diseased body and in childhood he will fear danger through snakes and water.* (BPHS 26:90)

This is a *Dainya Parivartana Yoga* (also a *Viparita Yoga*) wherein the lords are in a mutual 3/11 relationship from *trik* houses. As a consequence, the yoga may play out as a series of manageable crises.

The native has many competitors and enemies whom he defeats, such that they're more of a nuisance and a torment to him than a real menace. He is sexually aggressive, and attempts to form relations with women through promiscuous activity, adultery or rape.

Sickness is a major theme in life, and he goes through a number of health crises and recoveries. Viral infections, toxins or poisons cause problems in the bowels or the internal sexual organs. These may be difficult to diagnose, due to the hidden nature of their symptoms.

Maternal uncles and in-laws succeed through their own efforts, albeit with many setbacks, and make many short journeys.

Working life is fitful, with many breaks in employment, and there are difficulties with staff and co-workers, and bad working conditions. Typical occupations entail stealth in the face of opposition, eg, police or insurance investigation, medical or military research.

Other careers involve service in the face of traumatic events, eg, disaster relief teams, rape counselors, crime scene units, ambulance crews or critical care units, operating room staff, and hazardous materials handlers.

Famous people with this yoga

Prince Albert, British royalty; Paul Bowles, writer; Max Bruch, composer; Wilhelm Canaris, militarist; Robert Doisneau, photographer; Brendan Fraser, actor; W.D. Gann, astrologer/economist; Waylon Jennings, singer; Nathan Leopold, murderer; Jerry Lewis, comedian; Grandma Moses, artist; Martina Navratilova, tennis player; Emmy Noether, mathematician; Richard Petty, race car driver; Roman Prodi, educator; Gian-Franco Zeffirelli, director.

Case study

Martina Navratilova is a Czech-American tennis champion whom Billie Jean King once called "the greatest singles, doubles and mixed doubles player who's ever lived."

Born into a tennis-oriented family, she played her first tournament at age eight, the same year her father committed suicide. Off the court, she swam, skied, and played soccer and ice hockey, but nothing interfered with tennis.

She was stripped of Czech citizenship when, in 1975 at age 18, she asked the United States for political asylum and was granted temporary residency. Aside from speaking out on several volatile political issues, including litigation reform and gay/lesbian rights, she's been a vocal critic of Communism her whole life.

In her mid-20s she suffered from toxoplasmosis, an infection threatening the central nervous system. In her mid-40s she was treated for breast cancer, having a tumor surgically removed.

Public about being lesbian, she's been linked to several other prominent female athletes, one of whom engaged her in a bitter court battle over a palimony suit.

Navratilova is involved with various charities that benefit animal rights, underprivileged children and gay rights. She's written several books – a tennis instruction book, an autobiography, a fitness instruction book – and co-authored three mystery novels.

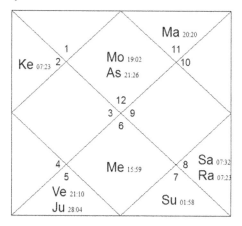

Venus in 6th house Leo exchanges with the Sun in 8th house Libra. Pre-exchange, Venus is ordinary, while the Sun is debilitated in Libra. Since each is a *trik* lord in a *trikisthana*, independent of the exchange, this forms the basis for a *Viparita Yoga*.

The 6th/8th exchange forming *Parivartana Yoga*, however, simply reinforces the *Viparita Yoga*, in which illness, trauma and litigation are potentially treated, resolved or defeated. We can see this in her life via successful recoveries from major health crises in her 20s and 40s, and in her dismissal of a palimony suit brought against her by a former companion.

Interestingly, Navratilova has a second *Parivartana Yoga*, the exchange of malefic enemies, 9th lord Mars and 12th lord Saturn. The most obvious problems from this quarter were loss of father through suicide, and legal problems regarding immigration.

Whereas the Sun is debilitated, Venus is merely ordinary, giving it the role of control planet in this exchange. Its position in the 6th house with *lagnesh* Jupiter speaks to both her competitive drive and her recovery from health crises.

Exchange of 6th and 9th lords

Parashara says:

- *If the 6th lord is situated in the 9th house, the native will trade in wood and stones and will confront fluctuations in trade.* (BPHS 26:69)

- *If the 9th lord is in the 6th house, the native will be less fortunate, be devoid of happiness from maternal uncle, etc, and be troubled by enemies.* (BPHS 26:102)

This is a *Dainya Parivartana Yoga* wherein the lords are in a mutual 4/10 relationship. As a consequence of this pattern, the yoga may reveal itself as a lack of luck in general, particularly in employment.

The native experiences setbacks in his spiritual pursuits. He questions his teachers or disagrees with elements of their belief system. His guru adopts an adversarial stand in order to test his resolve. His ethics may be questionable, such that he argues moral points of view, and gets into legal disputes.

The father's health is poor. Furthermore, the father's life entails a significant degree of struggle, with some blemish attached to his profession or reputation. By extension, the native's relationship with his father might be adversarial.

His maternal uncles or in-laws may be involved in the purchase or sale of vehicles or properties.

Competitors and enemies gain advantage over him. His employment situation fluctuates due to competition or the interference of others. Travel further exposes him to adversaries, and he suffers losses from foreign dealings. He has accidents or experiences ill health during journeys.

In terms of higher education, he does not favor religious subjects, and has difficulty achieving an advanced degree. He or his father is employed in medicine, law, defense or some aspect of foreign trade. Within the legal field, he may be an activist for animal or environmental issues.

Famous people with this yoga

Michele Alboreto, race car driver; Hans Christian Andersen, writer; Chris Carter, TV producer; Joe Clark, politician; John Cleese, actor; Tom Daschle, politician; Dr. Franz Hartmann, occultist; "Rocket" Ismail, football player; Kenneth Lay, corporate executive; Brenda Lee, singer; Auguste Piccard, scientist; William Pitt, British nobility; Edith Sitwell, writer.

Case study

John Cleese is an English actor, comedian and writer best known for his TV series, *Monty Python's Flying Circus* and *Fawlty Towers* ("I could run this hotel just fine, if it weren't for the guests.") and the movie, *A Fish Called Wanda*. Aside from his TV and movie roles, Cleese has also produced business training films using humor to make their points.

His family's surname was originally Cheese, but his father thought it embarrassing and changed it when he enlisted. Cleese blames his mother, who lived to 101, for his difficult relationships with women.

He was educated at Cambridge in mathematics, physics, and chemistry. For three years he was rector of the University of St. Andrew's, and held other similar posts at other universities.

Despite a career of poking fun at the establishment, he declined offers of peerage and to be made a Commander of the Order of the British Empire.

He's been married four times. He successfully sued a British tabloid for libel concerning an article about his sex drive, and donated the proceeds to a scholarship foundation. However, his divorce settlement to his third wife, an American psychotherapist, cost him over $20 million.

Politically involved and environmentally concerned, Cleese once declared, "I adore lemurs. They're extremely gentle, well-mannered, pretty and yet great fun. I should have married one."

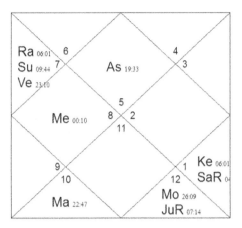

Mars in 6th house Capricorn exchanges with Saturn in 9th house Aries. By virtue of their special aspects, these two malefics and mutual enemies aspect each other, thus forming a *Dharma Karma Adhipati Yoga* via their rulership of the 7th and 9th houses.

All of the malefic planets in this chart occupy cadent houses. This implies some degree of (technical) prowess in the arts, in environmental issues, in academia.

Pre-exchange, Mars is exalted while Saturn is in a mixed state – retrograde but debilitated. Saturn is in mutual aspect with *lagnesh* Sun, which generates another *Dharma Karma Adhipati Yoga*. Saturn as a *kendra* lord with a node in a *trikona* also generates a *Raja Yoga*.

6th house themes have played out in problematic relationships, litigation and environmental causes. 9th house themes are evidenced in academic fields, legal matters and politics.

The cross-pollination of those two houses in exchange can be seen in his industrial/corporate training programs, as well as his declining social honors offered by the establishment.

Although Saturn is retrograde, it's also debilitated; meanwhile Mars is exalted, thus making it the control planet for this exchange. Mars in the 6th is the *agent provocateur*, the activist.

Exchange of 6th and 10th lords

Parashara says:

- *Should the 6th lord occupy the 10th house, the native will be illustrious in his family, will not be a devoted son, be a gifted speaker, and be happy in foreign countries.* (BPHS 26:70)

- *In case the 10th lord is fallen in the 6th house, the native will be bereft of paternal bliss, be bereft of wealth and be troubled by enemies in spite of being skillful.* (BPHS 26:114)

This is a *Dainya Parivartana Yoga* wherein the lords are in a mutual 5/9 relationship from *artha* houses. Because of this dynamic, the yoga will play out mainly in mundane, material, financial and employment arenas.

The native's life is made difficult by enemies who operate from a position of status. Advances in his career are slow and filled with obstacles, due to the influence of competitors. His social status may be threatened.

He has robust health, but may get sick or injured at work, either through a poisoned workplace or an occupational hazard.

His business fluctuates although, by dint of hard work, he makes steady gains in professional status, rising ultimately to a high level of accomplishment. If he is an employer or manager, his staff is very competent.

The person gets paid very well for work that is confrontational and/or traumatic. Occupations most favored are medicine and law, defense and police work. On a lower scale, many service occupations also offer relatively attractive pay rates because of the unsavory nature of the work, eg, butchers, garbage workers, environmental cleanup, etc.

Famous people with this yoga

Brendan Behan, playwright; Carlo Benetton, industrialist; Frank Capra, filmmaker; Edith Custer, astrologer; Linda Evans, actress; Lorne Greene, actor; Gary Middlecoff, pro golfer; Arantxa Sanchez-Vicario, tennis pro; Robert Sherwood, playwright; Karen Silkwood, activist; Heinrich Steinway, piano maker.

Case study

Karen Silkwood was an American chemical technician and labor union activist who raised concerns about corporate practices related to the health and safety of nuclear plant workers. She's most famous for her mysterious death, the subject of a victorious lawsuit against the chemical company. She gained more fame when she was portrayed by Meryl Streep in the Academy Award-nominated film *Silkwood*.

Married with three kids, Silkwood discovered her husband having an affair with her best friend, and left the family. She began working at a nuclear plant, became active in the workers' union and was elected to their bargaining committee, the first woman to achieve that position at the plant.

Concerned about unsafe working conditions at the plant, Silkwood gathered evidence and spearheaded a union effort to publicize the situation and make management accountable.

Exposed to radioactivity on-site, she was killed in a fatal car crash less than two weeks later under circumstances that strongly suggested foul play.

Her family later successfully sued her employer for negligence causing her death and, after judgment, appeal and review, received an out-of-court settlement of $1.4 million.

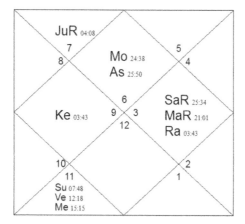

Mercury in 6th house Aquarius exchanges with Saturn in 10th house Gemini. *Lagnesh* Mercury is associated with Venus, forming both a *Dharma Karma Adhipati Yoga* and a *Dhana Yoga*.

Saturn is strong because retrograde. The association of 6th lord Saturn with 8th lord Mars constitutes a *Viparita Yoga*, albeit somewhat defused by the aspect of a retrograde Jupiter. The association of *trikona* lord Saturn in a *kendra* with a node also creates a *Raja Yoga*.

Note how *trikasthana* lord Mars, retrograde with *dig bala*, is eminently positioned to inflict harm via its aspects to both the ascendant and Moon.

The 6th house themes are strongly in evidence: dissolution of marriage, labor relations activism, concerns about the work environment, organized opposition, and legal action.

10th house themes are seen through corporate business, publicity and relative fame for actions (karma) taken.

Whereas Mercury is ordinary, Saturn is retrograde, giving it the strength to function as the control planet for this exchange. Thus, it borrows some muscle from Mars, some power from Rahu, and does its dirty work. Not all control planets are good for the owner of the chart. This is karma – the 10th house.

Exchange of 6th and 11th lords

Parashara says:

- *Should the 6th lord occupy the 11th house, the native will gain from his enemies, be virtuous, adventurous, honorable, but be bereft of progenic happiness.* (BPHS 26:71)

- *In case the 11th lord is posited in the 6th house, the native will generally remain sickly. He will be cruel, living in foreign places and be troubled by enemies.* (BPHS 26:126)

This is a *Dainya Parivartana Yoga* with the lords are in a mutual 6/8 relationship from *upachaya* houses. Due to this dynamic, themes of struggle and overcoming odds are dominant.

The native is not fortunate with job opportunities, and doesn't earn a high salary. His hopes and ambitions are hampered by competition, such that he eventually lowers his sights to diminished expectations. He makes gains through service occupations related to the medical, legal, or defense industries.

Although income isn't very good at the outset, it improves steadily with time. Similarly, although competitors are a torment, they too gradually diminish, such that he ultimately triumphs over them.

His health suffers from an early age, but gradually improves over time. Resistance to infections, especially in the bowel, is weak at first but eventually gets stronger.

His relationship with friends and elder siblings is strained. He faces competition from his sibling(s), and reversals of fortune among friends. Friends or elder siblings may have short or difficult lives.

Financial transactions among his friends turn out badly. Loans made to friends may go unpaid. Rough company may encourage him to seek illegal profits, especially if the planets involved in the exchange are malefics.

Famous people with this yoga

Gabriele d'Annunzio, writer; Indira Gandhi, politician; Karl Jaspers, philosopher; Quincy Jones, musician; Henri Pétain, statesman; Michelle Pfeiffer, actress; Ruth Pointer, singer; Walter Winchell, journalist; Peter Wolf, musician.

Case study

Indira Gandhi was India's only female Prime Minister (1966-1977) to date. Daughter of India's first Prime Minister Jawaharlal Nehru, she received an excellent education, studying history at Oxford and speaking perfect French.

During university, she was plagued with ill-health and constantly attended by doctors. Against her father's wishes she married a man who turned out to be an alcoholic and womanizer.

As Prime Minister, Gandhi was politically ruthless in centralizing her power. Although charged with electoral malpractice, jailed and banned from office, she staged a comeback. During India's state of emergency, she allowed her son Sanjay to create what was effectively a police state.

She was an advocate of equal pay for equal work. She presided over the nationalization of India's banking, coal, steel, copper, refining, textile and insurance industries, largely to protect employment and the interests of organized labor. She also orchestrated mass redistribution of land to assist the lower classes.

Gandhi unleashed a powerful military offensive in the 1970s, waging wars against Pakistan and East Pakistan, resulting in the partition of Bangladesh. She formed an alliance with Russia to the chagrin of America.

She was assassinated by two Sikh bodyguards whose loyalties changed after she used the army to dislodge militants from a Sikh holy site.

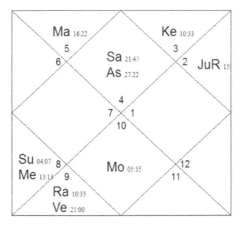

Venus in 6th house Sagittarius exchanges with Jupiter in 11th house Taurus. Jupiter is retrograde, therefore strong, and involved in a *Dhana Yoga* via its mutual aspect with the Sun.

The 6th house themes are evidenced in Gandhi's strong-arm tactics, exercise of police and military might, and concern for organized labor and the rural masses.

11th house issues played out via her political astuteness and social reforms, while the blending of 6th/11th themes were revealed in her fluctuating political fortunes, with friends and allies one day becoming opponents the next, and vice versa. This reversal of fortunes was epitomized by her death at the hands of her own Sikh bodyguards.

A key factor in Gandhi's 6th/11th exchange is the presence of the Rahu-Ketu axis running through her 6th and 12th houses. This invoked karmic past-life influences with respect to treachery and betrayals through friends and secret enemies. Without the nodal affliction, that "treachery" theme would not have emerged so dramatically.

Gandhi's chart is truly extraordinary in that it also contains two other *Parivartana Yogas* – the Moon and Saturn in a 1st/7th exchange, and the Sun and Mars in a 2nd/5th exchange. (40% of the population has one *Parivartana Yoga*, only 3% has two such yogas, and only 0.03% has three.)

Whereas Venus is ordinary, Jupiter is retrograde, thus confirming it as the control planet for this exchange. Its position in the 11th house is representative of her social ideals and political role.

Exchange of 6th and 12th lords

Parashara says:

- *In case the 6th lord is placed in the 12th house, the money is spent on vices, and the native is inimical to the learned and does violence to animals.* (BPHS 26:72)

- *If the 12th lord is fallen in the 6th house, the native will incur enmity with his own men, be given to anger, be sinful, miserable, and will traverse others' wives.* (BPHS 26:138)

This is a *Dainya Parivartana Yoga* (also a *Viparita Yoga*) wherein the lords are in a mutual 7/7 relationship from trik houses. This *sambandha* of mutual aspect also serves to strengthen (and aggravate) the significations of the exchange.

The native suffers from adversaries, both open and secret, but eventually escapes their persecution, or the enemies themselves are neutralized through incarceration or isolation. Spiritual liberation, or *moksha*, is a struggle, either because he's unaware of a spiritual dimension in his life, or because he doesn't make efforts to overcome his own inner problems.

He may have something of a sexual obsession, being frequently in search of fresh partners, including those in other relationships. Consequently, his sexuality may be a cause of stress, with subsequent ramifications through perversion, deceit, rape, and/or infection.

Maternal uncles or in-laws may have a short or difficult life. He may have disputes with in-laws, servants and tenants.

His health is affected to the degree that hospitalization may be required, but since the 6th is an *upachaya* house, recuperation comes eventually. He should get inoculated before traveling to the third world, since foreign viruses are a danger to his health.

He may find foreign employment in a service occupation. Alternatively, his employees or co-workers are foreign nationals. Employees may prove to betray or undermine him.

He borrows heavily to spend, and finds himself constantly juggling his finances in order to make ends meet. If he could control his spending on unwholesome vices, he might otherwise enjoy uninterrupted lifetime prosperity.

Famous people with this yoga

John Wayne Bobbitt, castration victim; Roger Elliot, astrologer; Georges Guynemer, military pilot; Joanna Lumley, actress; Dean Martin, entertainer; Odetta, singer; Tony Randall, actor; Jean-Paul Sartre, existentialist; Bruce Scofield, astrologer; Cybil Shepherd, actress; Taylor Swift, musician.

Case study

Taylor Swift is an American singer-songwriter whose debut album established her as a star. As of 2015, she's won seven Grammy Awards and many other industry awards.

Known for narrative songs about personal experiences, she's been described as "a songwriting savant." But she also has her critics, with one saying, "she's also a high-strung, hyper-romantic gal with a melodramatic streak."

Her love life, involving Joe Jonas, Taylor Lautner, John Mayer, Jake Gyllenhaal, Harry Styles and other celebs, has attracted inordinate media attention. The *New York Times* wondered if she was in the midst of a "quarter-life crisis," while a Baptist church labeled her "the whorish face of doomed America."

Whatever the circumstances, Swift has tried to defuse conflict. After the 2009 MTV awards when Kanye West said Beyoncé should have won her award, Swift told an interviewer that Kanye later offered a personal apology. She refused to discuss the incident in subsequent interviews so as not to make a bigger deal of it.

Less known than is her music or love life, Swift is an active philanthropist, donating to and performing on behalf of causes related to arts education, children's literacy, victims of natural disasters, LGBT rights, sick children and community affairs.

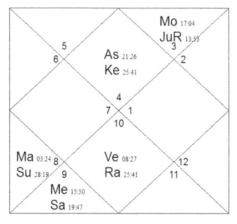

Mercury in 6th house Sagittarius exchanges with Jupiter in 12th house Gemini. Mercury and Jupiter, as *trik* lords, along with Saturn, form what is called a "full *mala*" in the formation of a *Viparita Yoga*, wherein all three *trik* lords occupy other *trik* houses.

Although it might be comforting to say it's the nature of *Viparita* to reverse/negate misfortunes, the fact remains that *lagnesh* Moon is associated with or aspected by all three *trik* lords. As such, it risks becoming the victim of collateral damage in the struggle among these three functional malefics. Although Swift has been blessed thus far with health, looks, talent, fame and fortune, life is long…

Although Mercury forms no other yoga, Jupiter before or after exchange retains contact with the Moon, resulting in both a *Dharma Karma Adhipati Yoga* and a *Kesari Yoga*, and with Saturn, generating another *Dharma Karma Adhipati Yoga*.

6th house themes have thus far been revealed through an irregular love life. In all fairness, Swift is only in her 20s, but this might well be an ongoing state of affairs.

12th house themes are evidenced through her extensive philanthropy and, to a lesser degree, her sex life that's become overly publicized in the media.

Whereas Mercury is ordinary, Jupiter is retrograde, making it the control planet for this exchange. Its placement in the 12th evokes her philanthropy.

For a more complete analysis of this chart, see the Taylor Swift article on my website navamsa.com.

EXCHANGES INVOLVING THE 7TH HOUSE LORD

Exchange of 7th and 8th lords

Parashara says:

- *In case the 7th lord happens to fall in the 8th house, the native will be bereft of marital happiness. His wife also will be afflicted by diseases, bad-natured, and will not remain obedient to the native.* (BPHS 26:80)

- *If the 8th lord is placed in the 7th house, the native will have two wives, and if he is in conjunction with a malefic planet also, there will certainly be loss in his trade.* (BPHS 26:91)

This is a *Dainya Parivartana Yoga* wherein the lords are in a mutual 2/12 relationship. Because of this dynamic, the yoga typically plays out in troublesome, irregular or traumatic dealings with significant others.

The native has difficult relationships that are spoiled by inconsistent behavior, dishonesty or greed. He has an unhappy marital life, and separation or divorce is a common outcome. The spouse is ill-tempered or psychologically flawed, either as a result of family traumas or other misfortunes in life.

The spouse is very interested in sex, occult practices or other mystical traditions, but has difficulty integrating these elements into her life. For instance, she may have problems with her reproductive system, or her sexual expression.

The spouse is sickly, undergoes surgeries, is afflicted by accidents, and has chronic physical complaints. In the extreme, these could be debilitating or life-threatening.

The native and his partner have problems with other people's money, and get into trouble through loans and debts. The partner could contribute to money problems through gambling or some other form of financial mis-management.

Alternatively, the partner may be professionally involved in the fields of banking, insurance, research or trauma management.

Famous people with this yoga

Lynn Anderson, singer; John Barth, writer; David Berkowitz, serial killer; Daniel Berrigan, activist; Barbara Bush, American First Lady; Jeb Bush, politician; Quentin Crisp, humorist; Willem Dafoe, actor; Phil Everly, musician; Fabio, model; Alberto Fujimori, politician; Sugar Ray Leonard, boxer; Billy Martin, baseball manager; Joseph McCarthy, politician; Audie Murphy, actor; Joe Namath, football player; Jerry Rubin, activist; Bertrand Russell, philosopher; Rusty Schweickart, astronaut; Sam Shepard, playwright; Peter Sutcliffe, "Yorkshire Ripper"; Zucchero, singer.

Case study

Bertrand Russell was a British-Welsh writer, mathematician, logician, philosopher and social activist, considered one of the 20th century's most important liberal thinkers.

Born into the British aristocracy, he became acquainted with death at an early age, with both parents and a sister dying by the time he was four. His adolescence was very lonely, and it was only his interest in mathematics that kept him from suicide.

He produced over 3,000 publications, authored more than 40 books, and won a Nobel Prize for Literature. But he was outspoken and controversial for his day. Anti-war protests landed him in prison during WW1, and 50 years later he was again briefly jailed for anti-nuclear protests.

Russell was an active supporter of homosexual law reform, calling for a change in the law regarding male homosexual practices. On another occasion, he was dismissed from a university post for his avant-garde views on sexual morality.

He once survived a plane crash, saying he owed his life to smoking since the people who died were in the non-smoking part of the plane.

He was married four times. During a separation period in his first marriage, he had passionate (and often simultaneous) affairs with a number of women.

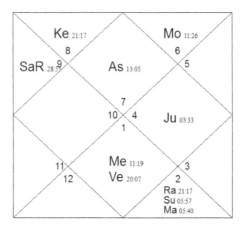

Venus in 7th house Aries exchanges with Mars in 8th house Taurus. Venus in the 7th constitutes *karako bhavo nashto*, wherein relationships are made vulnerable through affliction by either natal or transiting malefics.

Pre-exchange, *lagnesh* Venus associates with 9th lord Mercury to form *Dharma Karma Adhipati Yoga* while, as 8th lord, it combines with 12th lord Mercury for a *Viparita Yoga*. Mars in the 8th is weak, being totally combust within a 17-minute arc.

Pre- or post-exchange, the nodal axis afflicts 7th lord Mars or relationship *karaka* Venus, thus destabilizing marital status.

The 7th house themes of marriage, sex, war and activism were all dominant in Russell's life.

8th house themes arose through early acquaintance with death, thoughts of suicide, life-threatening accidents, scientific investigation and philosophical inquiry. Largely due to his stubborn adherence to ideals that ran counter to conventional morality, he also had more than his fair share of career reversals and public scandals.

Whereas Venus is ordinary, Mars is totally combust. This gives Venus the relative strength to function as the control planet in this exchange. Its placement in the 7th house speaks to his battleground in life – relationships, both personal and social.

Exchange of 7th and 9th lords

Parashara says:

- *If the 7th lord is situated in the 9th house, the native will have union with many women, be well disposed to his own wife, and will initiate a number of deeds.* (BPHS 26:81)

- *If the 9th lord is placed in the 7th house, the native will get happiness through his wife. He will be virtuous and famous.* (BPHS 26:103)

This is a *Maha Parivartana Yoga* (also a *Dharma Karma Adhipati Yoga*) wherein the lords are in a mutual 3/11 relationship. Because of this dynamic, the yoga typically unfolds via fortuitous relationships with significant others.

The native is healthy, attractive, respected, and fortunate in life. He enjoys a happy married life, with a spouse who is well-educated, spiritually inclined, and of a strong moral disposition. The spouse is also adventurous, artistic or athletic, and well-traveled. His spouse serves his father and/or her own brother, either through personal favors or employment.

He may pursue other relationships after marriage, although without the intention of replacing the spouse. He meets potential partners in the course of travel, in libraries and bookstores, or in places of learning and worship.

He travels in pursuit of a higher education, and develops relationships with people in the country that hosts him. He is successful in business and trade. Travel is significant, including periods of residence in a foreign country.

His father is financially successful, and enjoys a wide circle of friends. His father travels a lot and could die away from home.

Famous people with this yoga

Brendan Behan, playwright; Pat Buchanan, politician; George Carlin, comedian; Rubin Carter, homicide; Bruce Chatwin, travel writer; Adolf Eichmann, Nazi; Michael Erlewine, astrologer; Gary Hart, politician; Jack Nicholson, actor; Judge Reinhold, actor; Gerhard Schroder, politician; Dick Sutphen, mystic; Toni Tennille, singer; Sid Vicious, musician; Jerry West, basketball player; Walter Winchell, journalist.

Case study

George Carlin was an American comedian, social critic, actor and author who tackled politics, the English language, psychology, religion and various taboo subjects.

Although raised a Catholic, Carlin rejected it, and in his comedy often criticized religion, God and religious adherents. His later routines shifted to socio-cultural criticism of modern American society.

In his youth he joined the Air Force, working part-time as a radio station disc jockey, but was court-martialed three times and discharged for being unproductive.

After establishing himself as a standup comic, he became one of Johnny Carson's most frequent substitutes on *The Tonight Show*. Later he ran afoul of the FCC, charged with violating obscenity laws for "Seven Words You Can Never Say on TV."

He mixed observational humor with larger social commentary, eg, "When you're born, you get a ticket to the freak show. When you're born in America, you get a front-row seat."

His first hardcover book, *Brain Droppings*, sold 900,000 copies over 40 weeks on the *New York Times* bestseller list. When asked on *The Actor's Studio*, what made him proudest of his career, he said the number of books he'd sold.

His first marriage endured 36 years until his wife's death, and a second marriage lasted 10 years until his own death in 2008.

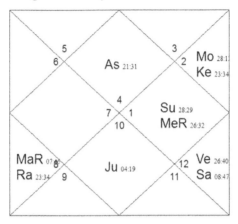

Jupiter in 7th house Capricorn exchanges with Saturn in 9th house Pisces. Jupiter is debilitated and participates in no other yoga. Saturn is ordinary and forms no other yoga.

7th house themes played out in a stable marital life, and a very interactive relationship with his fans (especially hecklers) during his live performances.

The 9th house topics found outlet in his legal issues (both private and professional), through his work in broadcast media and the publishing industry, and his penchant for poking fun at religion and undermining the establishment.

The 7th/9th exchange came full circle with the publication a few years after his death, with a collection of previously-unpublished writings and artwork by Carlin interwoven with his second wife's chronicle of their last ten years together.

Whereas Jupiter is debilitated, Saturn is merely ordinary, giving it the relative strength to function as the control planet for this exchange. Its placement in the 9th house reflected his success in broadcasting and publishing, as well as his frequent attacks on organized religion.

Exchange of 7th and 10th lords

Parashara says:

- *In the event of the 7th lord being placed in the 10th house, the native's wife will not remain under his control. The native himself will be religious and be gifted with wealth, sons, etc.* (BPHS 26:82)

- *If the 10th lord occupies the 7th house, the native will get happiness through his wife, be intelligent, virtuous, eloquent, truthful and devoted to religion.* (BPHS 26:115)

This is a *Maha Parivartana Yoga* wherein the lords are in a mutual 4/10 relationship from *kendra* houses. As a result of this dynamic, the yoga often manifests through an accomplished partner in life who enjoys public success of some sort, which may also benefit him.

The native is spiritually inclined and devoted to his religion or some noble cause. He has all the professional skills of a diplomat – able to develop rapport with others, to counsel and negotiate successfully, and to reach closure on business agreements.

He enjoys many gains from business and achieves a status beyond his immediate social circle. He profits from partnerships in general, some of which may be cultivated in the course of foreign travel. Professionally, he functions well as some sort of agent.

His spouse is helpful in business. She is career-oriented and ambitious, both for herself and for her spouse. She may be involved in transactions involving vehicles or property. She is inclined to be autonomous, self-employed or active in social circles, acquiring publicity, a good reputation and/or honors in her profession.

Famous people with this yoga

Truman Capote, writer; Valerie Harper, actress; Karl Jaspers, philosopher; Kitty Kelley, celebrity biographer; Joanna Lumley, actress; Cotton Mather, founder of Yale University; Richard Nixon, US President; Dr. Elaine Pagels, Biblical scholar; Francis Scobee, astronaut; George Steinbrenner, baseball owner; Bob Woodward, journalist.

Case study

Richard Nixon was the 37th President of the USA (1968-1974), and the only one to resign office, following the Watergate scandal.

Named after Richard the Lion-Hearted, he was raised in a Quaker household and overcame his innate shyness only later in life. He worked in the family business to pay his way through college.

He served in the US Navy during WW2, gaining a reputation as an accomplished poker player. Post-war, he was an active anti-Communist, participating in the House of Un-American Activities.

Despite his loss to Kennedy in 1960, amid allegations of Democratic vote fraud, Nixon refused to contest the election, fearing it would damage America's image. Later, for similar allegiance to the country, he chose resignation rather than impeachment after Watergate.

He faced near poverty after resigning, and was down to $500 when the David Frost interviews earned him $600,000. He later went on to author 10 books in his retirement.

Nixon had a complex personality, secretive and awkward, yet strikingly reflective about himself. He distanced himself from people and was very formal, wearing a coat and tie even when home alone. One biographer called him a "smart, talented man, but the most peculiar and haunted of presidents."

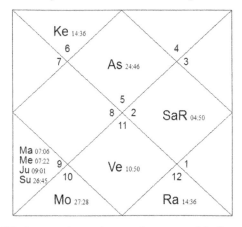

Venus in 7th house Aquarius exchanges with Saturn in 10th house Taurus. The two planets are mutual friends, but neither is involved in any other yoga. Saturn is powerful as a retrograde and, post-exchange, also obtains *dig bala*.

Perhaps because these are the only planets in *kendras*, their very isolation from others makes this *Parivartana Yoga* all the more potent and symptomatic of Nixon's life and career.

The 7th house is the place of relationships, marriage and diplomacy. Nixon was mutually devoted to his life-long spouse Pat whose support helped him in his career, and whose death deeply affected him.

With respect to the 10th house, his image has been mixed, quite literally. The media took delight in lampooning Nixon through caricatures, while Watergate cast a pall upon his reputation. As one biographer said, "How can one evaluate such an idiosyncratic president, so brilliant and so morally lacking?"

And yet history has acknowledged Nixon as perhaps America's greatest statesman. He brought the Vietnam War to an end, opened diplomatic relations with China, secured nuclear détente with the Soviet Union, and developed better relations with Latin America.

Whereas Venus is ordinary, Saturn is retrograde, thus granting it the strength to be the control planet for this exchange. Its placement in the 10th is symptomatic of both his hard-won rise to power and subsequent fall from office.

Exchange of 7th and 11th lords

Parashara says:

- *If the 7th lord occupies the 11th house, the native will gain wealth through his wife, will get less happiness from his sons, and will have more daughters (than sons).* (BPHS 26:83)

- *If the 11th lord is situated in the 7th house, the native always gains through his wife's relatives. He will be liberal, virtuous, sensual, and will remain at the command of his wife.* (BPHS 26:127)

This is a *Maha Parivartana Yoga* wherein the lords are in a mutual 5/9 relationship from *kama* houses. Thanks to this dynamic, the yoga often plays out through productive partnerships, whether personal, social or professional.

The native engages in business abroad and enjoys gains of foreign income. He is a natural networker, and strengthens his business relationships though partnerships, including with those of elder siblings.

He profits in some way through his spouse. For instance, the spouse will earn a good income of her own, or may come from a wealthy family. She may also provide introductions to an influential circle of associates that contribute to the native's prosperity. She is a romantic and an optimist, and is successful in speculation or games of chance.

The native's desire nature is strong and he experiences sexual attractions among his circle of friends, whether first-hand or through social media. He may be a member of a club, eg, Ashley Madison, dedicated to sexual liaisons.

The elder sibling is likely to pursue higher education in combination with foreign travel. Within the context of a dysfunctional family, an elder sibling could become romantically involved with the native's spouse.

Famous people with this yoga

Victor Borge, entertainer; Ron Howard, director; Neil Kinnock, politician; Mario Lanza, singer; Jack London, writer; Mike Love, musician; Ricky Martin, singer; Burgess Meredith, actor/director; Bill Wilson, founder of Alcoholics Anonymous.

Case study

Jack London was an American author, journalist, and social activist. A pioneer in commercial magazine fiction, he was one of the first writers to obtain worldwide celebrity and a large fortune from his fiction alone.

He was the son of an astrologer and a spiritualist. After one year of college, he dropped out and became a self-taught vagrant. He was an oyster pirate, joined the Klondike gold rush, roamed London's slums, savored his adventures and wrote them down.

He was an amateur boxer, an animal activist and a passionate advocate of unionization, socialism and workers' rights. He was a war correspondent for the 1904 Russo-Japanese War.

He was restless in his first marriage, sought extramarital sexual affairs, but later found in his second wife a sexually active, adventurous partner and life-companion.

London wrote 46 adventure tales that earned him world-wide fame, but he was constantly in debt. He was also a dissolute, with poor health (rectal ulcers, skin problems, kidney disease) compounded by unusual dietary habits (raw fish and meat), alcoholism and drug abuse, the latter of which killed him.

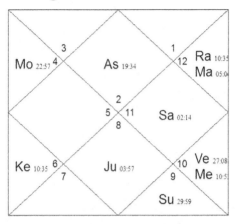

Jupiter in 7th house Scorpio exchanges with Mars in 11th house Pisces. The two planets are mutual friends but otherwise uninvolved in any other yoga.

The 7th house themes played out in a form of constructive vagrancy, wherein he traveled far and wide, engaging in risky adventures wherever he went: boxing, piracy, extra-marital affairs, use of prostitutes, and war correspondence. Kidney disease is also found under the 7th house.

The 11th house topics were epitomized by his social activism (advocacy of labor union movements, and animal rights long before they became popular), cutting a broad swath through society, enormous earnings for a writer of the day, and fame through his chronicled exploits. His work was said to reflect every tendency and big idea, and at one time he was considered the best-read writer in the United States.

In this case, both Mars and Jupiter are ordinary, and neither is involved in any yogas. We might therefore say there is no control planet for this exchange. If pressed, however, we could favor Mars because it is the more elevated. Its position in the 11th evokes his social activism, widespread popularity and huge earnings.

Exchange of 7th and 12th lords

Parashara says:

- *If the 7th lord is gone in the 12th house, the native will be penurious, miserly, and his wife will be spendthrift. He will earn his livelihood by trading in clothes, textiles, garments, etc.* (BPHS 26:84)

- *Should the 12th lord occupy the 7th house, the native will always expend on account of his wife, will not enjoy conjugal bliss, and will be bereft of learning and strength.* (BPHS 26:139)

This is a *Dainya Parivartana Yoga* wherein the lords are in a mutual 6/8 relationship. Under this dynamic, the yoga can manifest as impractical, illusory or self-destructive relationships

The native generally lives a troubled life, either as a result of illness, spending too much, having an unsatisfactory sex life, or being isolated from the people or things he cares for. He travels a lot and may take up foreign residence because of a love relationship. He incurs expenses for the sake of love and sex, primarily to please his partner, but also for personal indulgence, including the hire of prostitutes.

Marital life is unhappy due to sexual frustration, betrayal or poor health of the spouse. He is separated from his spouse by virtue of emotional disposition, physical distance, desertion or death. Prospects are poor for partnerships of all kinds, with business associates equally likely to part ways. Contractual agreements with business partners get broken, with debts and financial losses resulting.

His illnesses take the form of psychosomatic ailments, or real problems with kidneys or sexual organs, including STDs.

He has a great fascination for sexuality in all its forms, and his restless desire to experience variety will ultimately be a source of unhappiness. He may engage in secretive sexual behavior, or be partner to a secret sexual relationship. Spiritual liberation, or *moksha*, will therefore be elusive so long as he is trapped in an endless cycle of sexual relationships.

Famous people with this yoga

Eddie Arcaro, jockey; Gabriele d'Annunzio, writer; Betty Ford, American First Lady; Ernest Gallo, vintner; Dr. Albert Hoffmann, LSD chemist; Queen Latifah, singer; Liza Minnelli, actress; Vladimir Nabokov, writer; Pope John Paul II, ecclesiastic; Wilhelm II, German Emperor.

Case study

Liza Minnelli is an American actress and singer best known for the film *Cabaret* in which she won an Academy Award. She first performed on film at age three with her mother Judy Garland.

Primarily considered a pop singer, she's also appeared in several Broadway productions, movies and TV shows. Like Cher, she's considered both an American and gay icon. One critic said, "her every stage appearance is perceived as a victory of show-business stamina over psychic frailty."

Minnelli has long suffered from alcoholism, and has been addicted to prescription drugs. Struggling with substance abuse, she became one of the first prominent people openly talking about rehab.

She's been married (and divorced) four times. Her first husband was gay. Her 4th husband alleged that she beat him in alcohol-induced rages during their marriage. She's had three miscarriages, no children.

After a serious case of viral encephalitis, doctors predicted she'd spend the rest of her life in a wheelchair, perhaps never speak again. No stranger to hospitals, she's had two hip replacements, two knee surgeries, spinal fusion, a polyp removed from her vocal cords, and made emergency visits for suspected heart attack, dehydration and concussion.

Throughout her lifetime, Minnelli has served various charities she considers very important, especially AIDS.

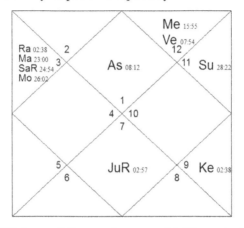

Jupiter in 7th house Libra exchanges with Venus in 12th house Pisces. Jupiter has strength via its retrogression. Venus is exalted. Neither forms any other constructive yoga.

Post-exchange, Venus in the 7th invokes *karako bhavo nashto* and the potential erosion of relationships.

7th house themes revealed themselves through her multiple marriages and other affairs with celebrities of the day.

But it's the 12th house that really looms large in doling out the troubles she's experienced in life: Valium addiction dating back to the traumatic death of her mother, alcoholism, institutionalization in rehab clinics for substance abuse, and hospitalization for a wide range of physical injuries and illnesses.

A more positive 12th house attribute is her involvement in charities for AIDS and children's brain development.

Although Jupiter is retrograde, its dignity is trumped by the exaltation of Venus, thus making it control planet for this exchange. Its placement in the 12th is symptomatic of her many misfortunes – through loss of loved ones, substance abuse, rehab and hospitalizations.

EXCHANGES INVOLVING THE 8TH HOUSE LORD

Exchange of 8th and 9th lords

Parashara says:

- *If the 8th lord is situated in the 9th house, the native will be a betrayer of his religion and a heterodox; he will be the husband of a wicked wife and will steal other's wealth.* (BPHS 26:93)

- *If the 9th lord is gone in the 8th house, the native will be devoid of fortune, and he will not have the happiness of an elder brother.* (BPHS 26:104)

This is a *Dainya Parivartana Yoga* wherein the lords are in a mutual 2/12 relationship. Because of this dynamic, typical manifestations include problems with the father and a distinct lack of luck in life.

The native follows an unorthodox religion or spiritual pursuit, and is inclined toward the so-called "left hand path" of occult studies, eg, sex magic, witchcraft and raising the dead. Alternatively, he pursues a conventional spiritual path but is misled by a false or unreliable guru. His morality is deficient, such that he tries to profit materially from those with whom he associates.

His general fortunes in life are largely obstructed, such that he can't capitalize on opportunities. "If it weren't for bad luck, I wouldn't have any luck at all." He has difficulty pursuing his higher education, and faces interruptions or changes in direction. Similarly, foreign travel encounters delays, cancellations, documentation problems and other complications. He is unsuccessful in legal proceedings.

Physically, he has problems with the hip, lower back and sciatic nerve. His father's health is poor, or his father is subject to accidents, surgeries and miscellaneous losses or mishaps in life. On the positive side, he may inherit his father's property.

His potential career path includes the fields of insurance, estate planning, and the administration of trusts and wills.

Famous people with this yoga

Piers Anthony, writer; Stephen Arroyo, astrologer; Nino Benvenuti, boxer; Jerry Brown, politician; Truman Capote, writer; Clint Eastwood, actor; Harlan Ellison, writer; Friedrich Engels, communist; Marvin Gaye, musician; D.W. Griffith, director; Larry Hagman, actor; Warren Harding, politician; Dustin Hoffman, actor; Bobby Hull, hockey player; Kris Kristofferson, musician; Moebius, cartoonist; Franz von Papen, politician; Sean Penn, actor; Sylvia Plath, writer; Pierre Salinger, journalist; Jon Voight, actor.

Case study

Sylvia Plath was an American poet, novelist, and short-story writer. Her father, a biology professor who wrote a book about bees, died of untreated diabetes when Plath was eight. Many of her later poems spoke of her love, hate, fear and fused identity with that of her father.

During university, furious at missing a chance to meet poet Dylan Thomas, she slashed her legs. Following shock therapy for depression, she took sleeping pills but survived after lying in a crawl space under her house for three days.

Although a brilliant writer, she was tortured by jealousy, obsessions and depression, finally learning "to be true to my own weirdness." She is credited with advancing the genre of confessional poetry.

After marriage to British poet Ted Hughes, they both became interested in astrology, the supernatural and Ouija boards. They had two children but, after he had an affair, they separated and she committed suicide by putting her head in a gas oven in 1963.

Posthumous publication of her last poetry book assured Plath's fame. Critics saw the collection as her increasingly desperate death wish. Radical feminists accused Hughes of abuse and threatened to kill him in Plath's name. Their son, following a history of depression, hanged himself in 2009.

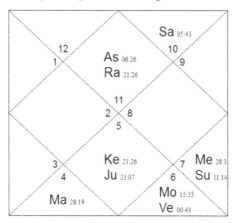

Venus in 8th house Virgo exchanges with Mercury in 9th house Libra. Pre-exchange, debilitated Venus forms no productive yoga with a dark Moon, and is hemmed by malefics the Sun and Ketu. Mercury forms *Dharma Karma Adhipati* and *Budhaditya Yogas* with the Sun.

The entwinement of 8th/9th themes is powerfully evidenced in Plath's complex feelings around love, despair, rage, vengeance, ambivalence, grief, death, redemption and resurrection, with father figures looming large in so much of her work. Depression, desperation and death wish are also bound up in the 8th.

Note that, not only is the 9th house "damaged" by the exchange with the 8th lord, but the house itself is heavily afflicted. The Sun, *karaka* for the father, is debilitated and aspected by malefics – a debilitated Mars from the 6th and a strong Saturn from the 12th – two mutual enemies whose opposition across the 6th/12th axis is itself a signature for self-harm and -undoing.

Since Venus is debilitated while Mercury is ordinary, this gives it the relative strength to function as control planet for this exchange. Mercury's placement in the 9th relates to her literary status and feminist legacy.

Exchange of 8th and 10th lords

Parashara says:

- *If the 8th lord occupies the 10th house, the native will not have paternal bliss, will be a tale bearer and be bereft of livelihood. If there is an aspect in the process from a benefic, then these evils will not mature.* (BPHS 26:94)

- *In case the 10th lord is posited in the 8th house, the native will be devoid of good acts, long-lived, and intent on blaming others.* (BPHS 26:116)

This is a *Dainya Parivartana Yoga* wherein the lords are in a mutual 3/11 relationship. The yoga often plays out through reversals in career or social status, thus affecting reputation.

The native has difficulty determining his right career and faces false starts and changes of direction. He uses all means, both fair and foul, to succeed in his career, but despite his best efforts, he encounters impediments and frequent setbacks.

He has difficulty with self-promotion, and is perceived as someone who lacks the drive or skills to succeed. Even when he performs his job well, he doesn't get credit for it, and less qualified people get promoted before he does. He may experience embarrassment in a public place, or his social reputation is soiled.

Appropriate career fields include banking and insurance, medicine and the healing arts, psychology and any other discipline dedicated to transformation of the individual. On a more mundane level, mining, salvage and trade in scrap or used articles are profitable activities.

Finally, for some, the business may be immoral or illegal, such as prostitution, theft, dealing in contraband or stolen articles, money laundering, etc.

Famous people with this yoga

Marcia Clark, prosecutor; Carrie Fisher, actress/writer; Paul Horn, musician; Queen Isabel I, Spanish royalty; Sally Kellerman, actress; Jim Lewis, astrologer; Trini Lopez, musician; Arthur Scargill, labor leader; Sylvester Stallone, actor/writer; Tina Turner, singer; Shania Twain, country artist; Rudolph Valentino, actor.

Case study

Tina Turner is a singer, actress, and author whose career has spanned over half a century. Noted for her energetic stage presence, powerful vocals and career longevity, the "Queen of Rock 'n' Roll" has won eight Grammy awards and sold more concert tickets than any other solo performer.

Born to sharecropper parents, her mother fled an abusive relationship, leaving Tina and her sister in the care of their grandparents. A self-professed tomboy, she was both a cheerleader and basketball player during high school.

Her music career began when she teamed up with Ike Turner. But after 16 years of physical abuse, along with his cocaine habit and blatant infidelities, she ran away with only 36 cents in her pocket. She had nose surgery to repair a septum damaged from Ike's frequent beatings, and at one time attempted suicide by swallowing 50 Valium.

Despite a near-fatal bout with tuberculosis, she transformed her solo career over six hard years. Although raised a Baptist, she later melded her faith with Buddhism, crediting the religion and its spiritual chant of *Nam Myoho Renge Kyo* with helping her through difficult times.

She later married a German music executive, renounced her American citizenship and became a Swiss national.

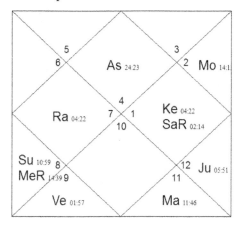

Mars in 8th Aquarius exchanges with Saturn in 10th house Aries. Neither malefic is involved in any other significant yoga. Saturn is in a mixed state, being both retrograde and debilitated, hemmed by benefics and closely aligned with the Rahu-Ketu axis.

Post-exchange, Mars gains *dig bala* in the 10th. Pre- or post-exchange, prime malefics dominate the angles.

Difficult 8th house themes are seen in Ike's cocaine addiction, her exposure to violence at his hands, her debts after splitting from him (leaving her responsible for cancelled tour dates), and the resurrection of her career from battered singer/spouse to dynamic solo act.

10th house themes are evidenced in her enduring legacy as a performer, having been inducted into the Rock and Roll Hall of Fame, listed in *Rolling Stone*'s Top 20 singers of all time, and her own star on the Hollywood Walk of Fame.

Whereas Mars is ordinary, Saturn is debilitated but retrograde, leaving us in a quandary as to which enjoys relative strength. Since Saturn is afflicted by the nodal axis while Mars is free of influence, we might safely consider Mars the more likely control planet for this exchange. Its placement in the 8th house speaks to her multiple traumas, but also her self-renewal and recovery.

Exchange of 8th and 11th lords

Parashara says:

- *Should the 8th lord be placed in the 11th house, the native will be devoid of wealth, be miserable in boyhood, but happy in later life, and if the 8th lord be in conjunction with a benefic, be long-lived.* (BPHS 26:95)

- *If the 11th lord is fallen in the 8th house, the native will suffer losses in his undertakings. He will be long-lived, while his wife will die before him.* (BPHS 26:128)

This is a *Dainya Parivartana Yoga* wherein the lords are in a mutual 4/10 relationship. The yoga typically manifests as financial irregularities and broken social relationships.

The native experiences many ups and downs in life, especially with respect to income. His hopes and ambitions are jeopardized by unforeseen circumstances. He sustains reversals and financial losses in his undertakings.

His longevity is good, and he recovers from accidents and surgeries. He has hearing problems on the left side, or problems with the left hand or arm.

Friends and elder siblings are a source of unhappiness, either in his relationship with them, or because they suffer misfortunes in their lives. Friends and elder siblings may be undependable, neglectful or abusive.

In the case of a second marriage, his wife's children (5th from the 7th) will be a source of unhappiness, through substance abuse, inadequate education, or financial mismanagement.

He is the beneficiary of family inheritance or insurance policies, although he may in turn lose a good portion of this windfall. He works in the insurance field or some other business related to death or trauma, although this is not highly-paid work.

Famous people with this yoga

Les Aspin, politician; Karen Black, actress; Princess Caroline, Monaco royalty; Jacques Chirac, politician; Michael Elliott, Olympic skier; Jean Luc Godard, director; Clifford Irving, writer; Virginia Johnson, sex therapist; Albert Kesselring, militarist; Josef Mengele, Nazi doctor; Gerhardus Mercator, cartographer; Ryan O'Neal, actor; Lee Harvey Oswald, assassin; Siegfried, illusionist; Lily Tomlin, comedienne; Al Unser, race car driver; Raquel Welch, actress; Natalie Wood, actress.

Case study

Virginia Johnson was an American sexologist, writer and co-founder of the Masters and Johnson Institute. She and William Masters established a research foundation to study the psychology and physiology of sex using volunteer subjects under laboratory conditions.

At age 16 Johnson had enrolled in college but dropped out, spending four years in a state insurance office. She returned to college, studied music and began a career as a vocalist, singing country for a local radio station.

She became a business writer for a newspaper, studied sociology but never finished her degree. While at university she was hired as a research assistant at the Department of Obstetrics and Gynecology.

There she met William Masters and together developed polygraph-like instruments to measure human sexual arousal and its phases – excitement, plateau, orgasm, and resolution.

Although "Masters and Johnson" became a household word, she had serious reservations about their Institute's program to convert homosexuals into heterosexuals. Showtime recently broadcast a TV drama series based on the biography *Masters of Sex*.

Johnson was divorced four times. The first marriage to a politician lasted two days. She married a much older attorney and divorced him. She married a bandleader for six years and two kids. She married William Masters and divorced him too.

Perhaps she never found resolution.

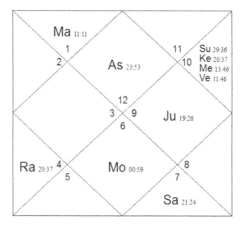

Saturn in 8th house Libra exchanges with Venus in 11th house Capricorn. Saturn is exalted and forms a *Dhana Yoga* with a strong Mars. Venus is ordinary but forms no constructive yoga.

Therefore, much rests on this *Parivartana Yoga* because, aside from the *Kesari Yoga* in *kendras*, there are few other yogas in this chart.

The 8th house themes are active via: early employment in the insurance industry, changes in studies, work in gynecology department, irregular marital life and divorce, scientific research applied to human sexual response, and (regrettably) experiments in sexual conversion.

Her 11th house themes are revealed through: a politician husband, a band-leader husband, radio work, her sociological studies and legacy, and the recent TV dramatization of Masters and Johnson, which has popularized their work all over again.

Whereas Venus is ordinary, Saturn is exalted, thus qualifying it as the control planet for this exchange. Its placement in the 8th house speaks to her legacy in matters of sexual research.

Exchange of 8th and 12th lords

Parashara says:

- *If the 8th lord be situated in the 12th house, the native will squander his wealth on evil deeds, be short-lived, more so if he is in conjunction with a malefic planet.* (BPHS 26:96)

- *In case the 12th lord is gone in the 8th house, the native will always have gains, will speak affably, will enjoy a medium span of life, and he will be endowed with all good qualities.* (BPHS 26:140)

This is a *Dainya Parivartana Yoga* (also a *Viparita Yoga*) wherein the lords are in a mutual 5/9 relationship from *trik* houses. Due to this dynamic, the yoga may manifest as a series of traumas and losses.

The native is drawn to spiritual life, but may be a dilettante incapable of consistent efforts in his practice. He's unable to sustain his pursuit of liberation, or *moksha*, because of distraction from sexual desires.

He has unanticipated expenses due to accidents, insurance claims, and psychological or medical problems. Alternatively, he prefers to spend his money on occult studies or sexual indulgences. He has a powerful sexual presence, with the ability to charm and seduce the objects of his desire, but he lacks sexual fulfillment and is in a state of constant craving.

Physically, he has problems with his feet, sexual or eliminative organs. His sleep is disturbed, or he gets no pleasure from sleep. His dreams may be upsetting.

Foreign residence is problematic for him, with unexpected misfortunes in the course of his stay. Alternatively, he may not like foreign cultures, or have difficulty interacting with foreigners. A certain degree of xenophobia may exist.

He has a heightened sensitivity, and may be intuitive, psychologically acute or psychic. On the flip side, he might suffer delusions or hear voices. He's likely to be isolated at some point in time, either voluntarily or involuntarily. On the positive side, this could mean retreat into seclusion, or time spent in an ashram. On the negative side, it could spell prison time, hospitalization or confinement to a mental institution.

Famous people with this yoga

Czar Alexander I, Russian royalty; Melvin Belli, attorney; William Holden, actor; Alan Leo, astrologer; Elizabeth Montgomery, actress; Santha Rama Rau, occult writer; Arantxa Sanchez-Vicario, tennis pro; Jack Swigert, astronaut/politician; Sharon Tate, actress; Usher, singer/actor; Edgard Varese, composer; Stevie Wonder, musician.

Case study

Melvin Belli was a prominent American lawyer known as "The King of Torts." Celebrity clients included Muhammad Ali, the Rolling Stones, Jim & Tammy Bakker, and Jack Ruby.

After law school, his first job was undercover investigator, riding the rails as a hobo to observe the Depression's effect on the country's vagrants.

Belli pioneered a jury-winning technique of dramatically demonstrating evidence, turning courtroom trials into theater, complete with props. He favored tailored suits, a red silk handkerchief and snake-skin boots.

His unprecedented use of graphic evidence and expert witnesses later became common courtroom practice. His principle of absolute liability, wherein manufacturers are automatically liable for injury caused by their products, set the stage for later consumer protection litigation.

After winning a case, he'd raise a Jolly Roger flag over his office building (formerly a brothel) and fire a cannon shot to announce a victory celebration.

Belli loved luxury homes, cars and yachts, travel and beautiful women. Most of all, he loved the law and authored 62 books, earning a successful second career on the lecture circuit.

Belli was married six times and divorced five. In his later years, he was enmeshed in legal battles, facing malpractice suits and owing a mountain of debts, including back taxes.

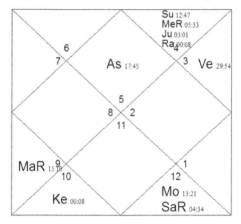

The Moon in 8th house Pisces exchanges with Jupiter in 12th house Cancer. The Moon forms a *Viparita Yoga* with Saturn. Jupiter is exalted and forms three yogas – a *Dharma Karma Adhipati Yoga* with the Sun, and two *Dhana Yogas* with Mercury.

The 8th/12th exchange is itself a form of *Viparita Yoga,* and the theme of "clouds with silver linings" was prominent in his career. His command of torts, or personal injury lawsuits, was instrumental in building his reputation. For every personal injury (loss) suffered by a client, there were potential damages (gain) to be sued from an employer or manufacturer.

But sometimes even such victories were hollow. Belli represented 800 women in a 1995 class action lawsuit against breast implant manufacturer Dow Corning. Belli won the case, but when Dow Corning declared bankruptcy, he couldn't recover the $5 million he'd advanced to doctors and expert witnesses, and was forced to file for bankruptcy protection.

Whereas the Moon is ordinary, Jupiter is exalted, thus making it the control planet for this exchange. Its placement in the 12th house reminds us that Belli's life's work was all about loss management – first, a client's suffering loss of wellbeing, but after successful litigation, loss imposed upon the manufacturer in damages awarded by the court.

EXCHANGES INVOLVING THE 9TH HOUSE LORD

Exchange of 9th and 10th lords

Parashara says:

- *If the 9th lord is placed in the 10th house, the native will be a king or equal to a king, or be a minister or an army chief, be virtuous and be worshipped by all.* (BPHS 26:106)

- *Should the 10th lord occupy the 9th house, the native is born in a royal family and becomes a king, while as an ordinary person he will be equal to a king. This combination confers on him wealth and progenic happiness.* (BPHS 26:117)

This is a *Maha Parivartana Yoga* (also a *Dharma Karma Adhipati Yoga*) wherein the lords are in a mutual 2/12 relationship. These are two of the most important and beneficial houses in the chart, and their reciprocal relationship is pivotal.

The 9th is the primary house of *dharma*, the 10th that of karma. Thus the yoga is bound to manifest via larger-than-life issues involving ethics, right action, personal belief systems, worldly effort, social reputation and fame.

The native is lucky and successful in life, with authority and high social reputation. He has a strong *dharma*, with an inclination to do the right thing and, thanks to good karma in this life, the things he does turn out well.

He receives a higher education in religion, ethics or philosophy, and travels extensively in pursuit of his studies. He acquires a teacher, mentor or guru who is well-known, accomplished and/or revered.

His father is successful, educated, wealthy, well-known and influential in some way that influences the native's career choice. His father may have a strong voice, whether literally in oratory or singing, or figuratively, as a public voice in politics.

This exchange favors a career in academia, publishing, government and the law, or provides benefits through association with such fields. In whatever career, the native appears to enjoy fortuitous circumstances that contribute to his success.

Famous people with this yoga

Richard Bach, writer; Kurt Browning, figure skater; Cesar Chavez, labor leader; Caryl Chessman, serial killer; Deepak Chopra, author; Karl Doenitz, militarist; Albert Einstein, scientist; David Frost, TV personality; King George III, British royalty; Mark Hamill, actor; Geri Halliwell, pop singer; John Higgins, snooker player; Peter Jennings, journalist; Ferruccio Lamborghini, automaker; Courtney Love, musician; Bela Lugosi, actor; Tracy Marks, astrologer; Joe Montana, football player; Marcia Moore, astrologer; Clifford Odets, playwright; Roy Rogers, actor; Will Rogers, humorist; Murray Rose, Olympic swimmer; Charles Starkweather, mass murderer; Harry S. Truman, US President.

Case study

Albert Einstein was a German-born theoretical physicist who developed the general theory of relativity, paving the way for 20th century physics and providing the essential structure of the cosmos. He won the 1922 Nobel Prize for his contributions to theoretical physics.

He was born with a misshapen head and abnormally large body. He learned to talk so late his parents feared he was retarded, and he wasn't fluent until he was nine.

After renouncing German citizenship, he took a post at the Swiss patent office where he worked on his theory of relativity. $E=mc^2$ was since dubbed "the world's most famous equation."

He moved to the USA and accepted a teaching post at Princeton University. He published over 300 scientific papers and 150 non-scientific works. His intellectual originality made "Einstein" synonymous with genius. He spent his final years working on a unified field theory.

Married and divorced from his first wife, he promised his future Nobel Prize money as part of her alimony. A musician by hobby, he gave up the violin in the last few years of his life, but enjoyed playing Bach and Mozart on his grand piano.

Einstein was a passionate, committed pacifist, socialist and anti-racist.

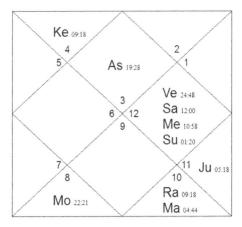

Jupiter in 9th house Aquarius exchanges with Saturn in 10th house Pisces. Jupiter is hemmed by malefics but otherwise participates in no other yoga. Saturn is part of a large stellium that includes the Sun with *dig bala*, exalted Venus and debilitated *lagnesh* Mercury, with which it forms two *Dharma Karma Adhipati Yogas*.

Saturn and the three other planets in the 10th also form a *Pravrajya Yoga*. Although Einstein wasn't a particularly religious man, he was more spiritual than secular, witness his preference to remain in academia rather than accept an offer to become the first President of Israel.

9th house themes played out in his prestigious professorships in England and America, his theoretical work, and his cosmology.

10th house themes include honors and recognition via the Nobel Prize, public demand for speaking engagements, and his world-class reputation as a scientific genius.

Since both Jupiter and Saturn are ordinary, we might think of them as coequals. However, we could also weigh their relative importance in the chart. Because Saturn forms two *Raja Yogas* with *lagnesh* Mercury, we can judge it to be the control planet for this exchange. Its placement in the 10th reflects his huge and lasting status as a scientist.

Exchange of 9th and 11th lords

Parashara says:

- *Should the 9th lord be situated in the 11th house, the native will have financial gains day by day, be devoted to his teachers, virtuous, and be doer of charitable deeds.* (BPHS 26:107)

- *If the 11th lord happens to be placed in the 9th house, the native will be fortunate, skillful, truthful, honored by the King, and wealthy.* (BPHS 26:129)

This is a *Maha Parivartana Yoga* (also a *Dhana Yoga*) wherein the lords are in a mutual 3/11 relationship. Because of this dynamic, there is a bias for communication, teaching and courageous (right) action within a larger social context, whether artistic, business or political.

The native is successful in his spiritual pursuits, and has a guru who is a spiritual leader, with whom he develops a relationship like a friend. He receives honors and is held in high esteem by friends and social organizations. His friends, who may include clerics, lawyers, philosophers, professors and writers, are lucky and successful.

His father is athletic, fortunate, wealthy, intellectual, sociable, and makes many short journeys. His elder siblings are very fortunate in life, enjoying good incomes and achieving their ambitions.

He is very lucky in financial matters, and makes money through activities requiring relatively little effort, eg, through stock market investment, lotteries and other games of chance, or businesses that generate inordinate profits. He finds fortune in fields of publishing, law, travel, social media and the entertainment industry.

Famous people with this yoga

Honoré de Balzac, writer; Jeanne Calment, record longevity (122+ years); Gustave Courbet, artist; Catherine Deneuve, actress; Robert Downey Jr., actor; Roger Elliot, astrologer; Peter Hurkos, psychic; Al Jardine, musician; Moses Ben Maimon, philosopher; Steve McQueen, actor; Alfred de Musset, playwright; Ricky Nelson, singer; James Polk, politician; Erwin Rommel, militarist; Donald Rumsfeld, Defense Secretary; Queen Victoria, British royalty.

Case study

Erwin Rommel was a German Field Marshall in WW2, dubbed the "Desert Fox" for his success with the Afrika Korps. He'd originally considered becoming an engineer but joined the military at the request of his headmaster father, who'd served in the artillery.

In WW1, Rommel earned a reputation for courage and quick decisions, was wounded three times, and highly decorated. His war diaries became highly regarded by Hitler.

Between wars, he headed the War Academy and wrote a textbook on military tactics. He believed commanders must suffer whatever hardships front-line soldiers faced, for the sake of troop morale.

Rommel's marriage was happy, and he wrote his wife a letter every day while in the field.

In the invasion of France, his tank division became known as the "Ghost Division" because its rapid advances placed it so far forward that their actual position was unknown.

He was regarded a humane and professional officer. His Afrika Korps was never accused of war crimes, and captured Allied soldiers were treated well. During his time in France, he disobeyed Hitler's orders to deport Jews.

His criticism of SS brutalities implied involvement in a failed attempt to assassinate Hitler. Because Rommel was a national hero, Hitler had to eliminate him quietly. Faced with court martial, Rommel chose forced suicide by cyanide.

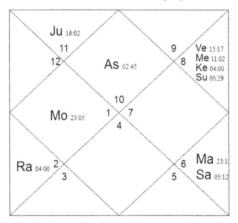

Mars in 9th house Virgo exchanges with Mercury in 11th house Scorpio. Mars associates with *lagnesh* Saturn to form a *Dharma Karma Adhipati Yoga* and a *Dhana Yoga*. Mercury associates with *yogakaraka* Venus to create another *Dharma Karma Adhipati Yoga*.

9th house themes are strongly in evidence: his father's academic and military experience, his own publications in tactical theory, his command of a military academy, and his profound moral courage in defying Hitler's Nazi doctrine.

11th house themes played out in spectacular successes over the course of two wars, popularity among his own troops, grudging respect from his military opponents, posthumous fame through the well-received movie *The Desert Fox*, and other honors, eg, having a museum in Germany named after him.

Both Mars and Mercury are ordinary. But Mars forms two yogas with *lagnesh* Saturn while Mercury forms only one with Venus. (If we look for a military analogy, we might note that Mars occupies higher ground.) Thus, Mars may be judged the control planet for this exchange. Its placement in the 9th speaks to the moral code of an honorable warrior, for which Rommel was loved by his troops and country, and admired by his enemies.

Exchange of 9th and 12th lords

Parashara says:

- *If the 9th lord is situated in the 12th house, the native will incur loss of fortunes, will always spend his money on auspicious acts, and will become poor because of spending money on entertaining guests.* (BPHS 26:108)

- *Should the 12th lord occupy the 9th house, the native will dishonor his teachers, be inimical even to his friends, and be always intent on achieving his own ends.* (BPHS 26:141)

This is a *Dainya Parivartana Yoga* wherein the lords are in a mutual 4/10 relationship. Due to this dynamic, the yoga may manifest as something of a morality play, wherein disregard of ethics or universal law causes a person to undermine his own life and thus become his own worst enemy.

The native has a strong interest in personal development, travels in pursuit of academic or spiritual studies, and acquires a foreign guru. He spends money on seemingly worthwhile causes such as education, charity and support of his guru. However, unless he has exercised good moral judgment, some of these monies could be ill-spent on wrong causes.

His father is a religious or spiritually-inclined man, but is psychologically distant, in poor health, or physically far from home. He may be engaged in unethical transactions involving vehicles or properties (the 12th is 4th from the 9th).

The native is engaged in business abroad, undertakes long and beneficial travels, and assumes foreign residence. Due to his desire to achieve his own ends and no other, he may bring discredit upon both himself and his teachers. In the worst case, he may commit a crime and be imprisoned or otherwise restrained because of his actions.

He is unlucky, except in sexual matters, where he enjoys wide experience, but remains ultimately unsatisfied.

Famous people with this yoga

Ann-Margret, actress; Bo Derek, actress; Glenn Ford, actor; Dorothy Hamill, figure skater; George Roy Hill, director; Eric Idle, actor; Marsha Mason, actress; Matthew McConaughey, actor; Martina Navratilova, tennis player; Tom Selleck, actor; Tom Waits, musician; Loretta Young, actress.

Case study

Tom Waits is an American singer-songwriter, composer and actor. One critic described his distinctive voice "like it was soaked in bourbon, hung in the smokehouse, then taken outside and run over with a car."

Waits' atmospheric lyrics, written in a cynical and pessimistic tone, frequently portray grotesque and seedy characters and places. Although his albums have found mixed commercial success in the USA, they've occasionally achieved gold in other countries.

After military service with the US Coast Guard, he began his career in the LA music scene. He put together a touring band, The Nocturnal Emissions, to cover everything from sleazy strip-show blues to supercilious lounge lizardry. He lived in motels for years, eating bad food and drinking too much.

One critic wrote, "A sympathetic chronicler of the adrift and downtrodden, Waits creates three-dimensional characters who, even in their confusion and despair, offer insight and startling points of view."

Waits has won, sometimes with substantial settlements, several lawsuits against advertisers using his material without permission. Separately, he also won a lawsuit against the LAPD.

Waits has donated some of his legal settlements to charity. A limited edition book of poems raised $90,000 for a local food bank.

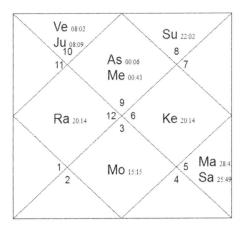

Mars in 9th house Leo exchanges with the Sun in 12th house Scorpio. These two malefics are friends and, for this chart, lords of *dharma* houses. Mars forms a *Dhana Yoga* with Saturn, while the Sun is isolated.

9th house themes have played out in a schoolteacher father who taught a foreign language, a mixed bag of luck in life, high principles (for some things), a philosophical turn of mind, foreign travels and successful lawsuits.

12th house themes are evident in his years of addiction, his rootless wandering, his greater professional success abroad than at home, and his donations to charitable causes.

Even his touring band's name, *The Nocturnal Emissions*, suggests all of the hallmarks of the 12th house – pleasures of the bed, sleep, sex, dreams, and unconscious release.

Both the Sun and Mars are ordinary, but whereas the Sun is isolated, Mars forms a yoga with Saturn, thus giving it the edge for control planet of this exchange. Its placement (with Saturn) in the 9th reflects Waits' cynical and pessimistic philosophy.

EXCHANGES INVOLVING THE 10TH HOUSE LORD

Exchange of 10th and 11th lords

Parashara says:

- *If the 10th lord is situated in the 11th house, the native is blessed with wealth and sons. He will enjoy happiness, be truthful, be always delighted, and be virtuous.* (BPHS 26:119)

- *Should the 11th lord be situated in the 10th house, the native will be honored by the king, be virtuous, devoted to his religion, truthful, and subdue his senses.* (BPHS 26:130)

This is a *Maha Parivartana Yoga* wherein the lords are in a mutual 2/12 relationship. The yoga may manifest in the entertainment, political, or arenas, through successful investments and resultant income.

The native has a successful career, a good reputation and is happy with his status in life. He thinks big and thrives in large corporate environments. He is well connected with people who enjoy business success and political influence.

He is fortunate in being able to fulfill his ambitions and materialize his dreams, and has the ability to inspire others to do the same. This favors careers in entertainment, inspirational speaking, financial management and social media.

He achieves prosperity through business with the help of friends or elder siblings. Ironically, his elder siblings suffer losses at the hands of secret enemies.

Because the lord of the 10th, the *karma karaka*, is in the 11th from whence it aspects the 5th house, the individual is capable of restraining his mind and his senses to obey his will. As the *shastras* suggest, "He will subdue his senses."

Famous people with this yoga

Mose Alison, musician; Princess Anne, British royalty; Josephine Baker, entertainer; Mike Bloomfield, musician; Bill Bradley, politician; Charles Bronson, actor; George Bush Sr., US President; Olivia DeHavilland, actress; Alan Dershowitz, lawyer; Glenn Ford, actor; George Gershwin, composer; Elliott Gould, actor; Graham Greene, writer; Gaylord Hauser, food advocate; George Roy Hill, director; Kirk Kerkorian, entrepreneur; Amyr Klynk, adventurer; Grant Lewi, astrologer; Marcello Mastroianni, actor; Joan Miro, artist; Brian Mulroney, politician; John Nash, mathematician; Sydney Omarr, astrologer; Roman Polanski, director; William Rehnquist, jurist; Susan Sarandon, actress; Elvis Stojko, figure skater; Jack Welch, corporate executive.

Case study

Josephine Baker was an American-French singer and entertainer. Nude on stage, she was an ebony statue – sexy, dazzling and exotic. Paris adored her. Hemingway called her the most sensational woman anybody ever saw or ever will.

Raised in poverty, she worked in white homes, sleeping in the basement with the dog. After being discovered street dancing, she went to New York and was billed as "the highest-paid chorus girl in vaudeville."

On a Paris tour, she became an overnight sensation, wearing only a skirt of bananas. She had a gift for communicating with the audience. Her jungle elegance onstage was complemented by her pet cheetah.

Fluent in French, German, Italian and English, during WW2 she was an Allied spy. Post-war, she refused to perform for segregated audiences in America, and was once offered unofficial leadership in the Civil Rights Movement.

She was married four times and adopted a "rainbow tribe" of 12 kids from all over the world. Her son claimed she was bisexual. After decades of wealth, she became extravagant and lost everything. Princess Grace arranged a house for her in Monte Carlo. After a heart attack, she recovered to make a triumphal return to the stage, but died four days later of a cerebral hemorrhage.

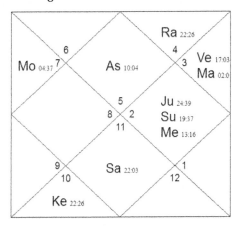

Mercury in 10th house Taurus exchanges with Venus in 11th house Gemini. Mercury forms a *Budhaditya Yoga* and two *Dhana Yogas* with the Sun, and another two *Dhana Yogas* with Jupiter. Venus forms a *Dharma Karma Adhipati Yoga* with Mars.

10th house themes are evident via her immense public popularity, her tremendous social rise "from a wild little dancer with a decent voice to a magnificent diva," and to her activism regarding the cause of desegregation in America.

11th house themes are revealed through troupe performance, robust income, social connections (Grace Kelly, Hemingway, Georges Simenon, Castro), and the civil rights movement.

Whereas Mercury is combust, Venus is merely ordinary, its relative strength making it the control planet for this exchange. Its placement in the 11th house reflects her status as a performing artist with a passion for the civil rights movement.

Exchange of 10th and 12th lords

Parashara says:

- *If the 10th lord is placed in the 12th house, the native will spend in royal courts. He will also have fear from enemies and will be worried in spite of being skillful.* (BPHS 26:120)

- *If the 12th lord is situated in the 10th house, the native will rise through royal persons and will enjoy only moderate paternal bliss.* (BPHS 26:142)

This is a *Dainya Parivartana Yoga* wherein the lords are in a mutual 3/11 relationship. The yoga may reveal its effect through scandal or unwelcome publicity, whether personal or professional.

The native is torn between the pursuits of spirituality and his career, and will therefore suffer frustrations in both. "One cannot worship Lakshmi and Saraswati under the same roof." Since his goals are more spiritual than mundane, he is disinclined to work hard for materialistic gain.

He has difficulty finding his true career, and experiences reversals in his profession, losses in business, and general unhappiness in his career. His profession may involve isolation or rehabilitation, such as in hospitals, sanitariums, correctional institutions, or ashrams. Some aspect of his job causes worry or unrest, contributing to insomnia.

His sexual reputation is exposed to the public eye, or his career may be somehow related to sexuality.

He works for a multi-national company, or takes up foreign residence because of his career. Alternatively, his career may involve import/export or immigration. He has many expenses or losses in business through foreign exchange, tax deductions, customs duties or government penalties.

Famous people with this yoga

Sir Claude Auchinleck, militarist; Bela Bartok, composer; Craig Breedlove, race car driver; Dick Cavett, talk show host; Teilhard de Chardin, paleontologist; Samuel Taylor Coleridge, poet; Kim Kardashian, reality show celeb; Bobby Knight, basketball coach; Alfred Von Krupp, industrialist; Janet Leigh, actress; Herman Melville, writer; Friedrich Nietzsche, philosopher; Arthur Schopenhauer, philosopher; Charles Steinmetz, scientist; Kiefer Sutherland, actor; Lee Trevino, golfer; Brenda Vacarro, actress.

Case study

Friedrich Nietzsche was a German philosopher and cultural critic who wrote on religion, morality, contemporary culture, philosophy and science. His most important ideas, will to power and the Superman, champion the creative powers of the individual to strive beyond social, cultural, and moral contexts.

Brought up in a strict Christian home, he was plagued by illnesses as a child, including migraines, violent indigestion, and moments of shortsightedness that left him nearly blind. He served as a medical orderly in the Franco-Prussian War, contracting diphtheria, dysentery and, possibly, syphilis.

Although granted a university teaching post at age 24 he abandoned it to spend a decade traveling Europe, during which time he wrote his important works. He rubbed shoulders with cultural heavyweights of the era – Richard Wagner, Rudolf Steiner, August Strindberg – but never achieved in public popularity the recognition bestowed by his peers.

His mental degeneration, brought on by syphilis or its contemporary cure mercury, resulted in delusions of grandeur and multiple personalities. He was declared insane and incarcerated for 11 years in a vegetative state until his death.

He never married. One theory suggests he was a homosexual in an era with no outlets. Separately, there was rumored incest with his sister. Ironically, she edited his last posthumous book, perverting his ideas to support Nazi doctrine.

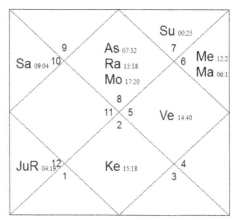

Venus in 10th house Leo exchanges with the Sun in 12th house Libra. The Sun – debilitated, *sandhi* and afflicted – forms no yoga. Venus is equally isolated. Post-exchange, the Sun gains *dig bala*.

Although the astrological reasons for Nietzsche's enduring contribution to philosophy are found elsewhere, the 10th house themes played out in more modest ways:

Early on, he was introduced to society through school where many of his classmates came from the best families. He achieved honors in his studies and critical acclaim for his ideas. He desired larger recognition but was reduced in the end to a megalomania wherein he ranked himself with other geniuses like the Buddha, Alexander the Great, Caesar, Voltaire, and Napoleon.

12th house themes can be seen in frequent illness and convalescence throughout his life, his 10-year wandering throughout Europe, unknown sex life, mental derangement and his 11-year incarceration in an asylum.

The Sun is debilitated whereas Venus is merely ordinary, giving it the relative strength to function as control planet for this exchange. Its placement in the 10th, despite his own diminished expectations, reflects his lasting reputation.

EXCHANGES INVOLVING THE 11TH HOUSE LORD

Exchange of 11th and 12th lords

Parashara says:

- *Should the 11th lord occupy the 12th house, the native will always expend on good deeds, be sensual, will have many wives, and will have friendship with barbarians or foreigners in general.* (BPHS 26:132)

- *In case the 12th lord is placed in the 11th house, the native will incur losses, in spite of having a combination of gains, and sometimes has meager gains through another's wealth.* (BPHS 26:143)

This is a *Dainya Parivartana Yoga* wherein the lords are in a mutual 2/12 relationship. Because of this dynamic, the yoga will typically produce unrest in the realms of friendship, group activity and financial matters.

The native enjoys a handsome income, but income and expenses go hand in hand, such that he finds it difficult to save money, and is at constant risk of significant debts. He has foreign sources of income, but incurs expenses related to foreign exchange, customs duties or transport that erode his profits. Personal expenses are generally for good causes, such as support of friends, elder siblings or children.

His close personal relationships are inconsistent, such that some friends become very close, while others become enemies. Included among his friends are foreigners, spiritual seekers or bohemian types. He is lucky in fulfilling his sexual desires, and has a wide circle of lovers, some of whom are less than reputable.

He may have an elder sibling who pursues spiritual liberation, or *moksha*. The sibling has little aptitude for financial management, and frequently incurs money problems, for which the native may assume responsibility.

Famous people with this yoga

Boris Becker, tennis player; Marc Bolan, musician; Fritjof Capra, physicist; Jimmy Carter, US President; Tony Curtis, actor; Salvador Dali, artist; Robertson Davies, writer; Michael Douglas, actor; Sir Arthur Conan Doyle, writer; Richard Harris, actor; Jesse Helms, politician; Jimi Hendrix, musician; Michael Hutchence, singer; Glenda Jackson, actress; Immanuel Kant, philosopher; Guglielmo Marconi, scientist; Guy de Maupassant, writer; Sal Mineo, actor; L'Wren Scott, fashion designer; Upton Sinclair, writer; Meryl Streep, actress; Dr. Ruth Westheimer, radio shrink; Sir George Wilkins, explorer.

Case study

Dr. Ruth Westheimer is an American sex therapist, media personality and author best known as Dr. Ruth. She ushered in the new age of franker talk about sex on radio and television, and has been endlessly parodied for her enthusiasm and an accent only a psychologist could have.

After her father was arrested by the Nazis in pre-WW2 Germany, she was sent away to take refuge in a Swiss orphanage. She lost contact with her family and presumed they'd died in Auschwitz. At age 17 she immigrated to Israel and subsequently lost her virginity. She fought for Israel's independence movement and was badly wounded in the foot.

She studied and taught psychology at the Sorbonne before immigrating to New York where she earned a master's degree in sociology and completed post-doctoral work in human sexuality.

After being discovered giving public lectures on sex, she was invited to join a late-night radio talk show. Its instant popularity eventually resulted in syndication, and in due course she gained a syndicated TV show.

She's appeared in several TV shows, for children and adults, and in a number of commercials, often using her brand name to comic effect. She's also written three books on sex.

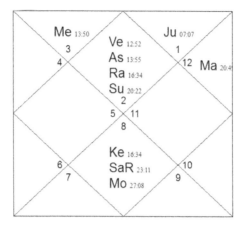

Mars in 11th house Pisces exchanges with Jupiter in 12th house Aries. These two planets are friends in an ordinary state, although Jupiter is hemmed by malefics. Neither Mars nor Jupiter forms any contact or yoga with any other planets save each other, likewise, in their post-exchange positions.

In Dr. Ruth's life, 11th house themes emerged with her involvement in political action for an independent Israel, her sociological studies, and her embrace of one of the earliest form of "social media" – radio.

12th house themes are present as well, in the loss of her family, seeking refuge in exile, immigration several times over, injury to the feet, studies in psychology, and in her dedication to shining a light on one of the most private experiences of human life.

Both Mars and Jupiter are ordinary, and form no other yogas. In this exchange, we might acknowledge there is no control planet, and the two will function as coequals. Their placement in the 11th and 12th, respectively, suggests her courage in using a public medium to counsel people in matters of sex.

Appendices, Bibliography, Case Studies

Appendix 1: *Avasthas*

Table 1: *Avasthas*

Avastha	Descriptive meaning	Technical meaning
Pradipta	Exulting, blazing	Exaltation sign
Sukhita	Happy	*Moolatrikona* sign
Svastha	Own	Own sign
Mudhita	Delighted	Sign of a friend
Shanta	Peaceful	Sign of a natural benefic
Shakta	Powerful, capable	Retrograde
Khala	Base, low	Sign of a natural malefic
Vikala	Imperfect, marred	Sign of an enemy
Nipidita	Tortured, defeated	Planetary war
Atibhita	Very frightened	Debilitated
Sudhuhkita	Very distressed	Combust
Kopa	Infirm, eclipsed	Eclipsed

Terms & definitions

Svastha (swa)

A planet's own sign is that which it is deemed to rule, and in which it feels comfortable, exerting its natural attributes with strength. See Table 2 below.

Moolatrikona

For planets owning two signs, the *moolatrikona* sign is considered to be the one in which the planet shows its best colors. General rule: a planet's *moolatrikona* sign is the male (air or fire) sign of its male/female pair. So for Mars, Jupiter,

Venus and Saturn, their *moolatrikona* signs are respectively Aries, Sagittarius, Libra and Aquarius. The only exception is Mercury, whose *moolatrikona* sign is Virgo. See Table 2 below.

Exaltation

Each planet has a sign in the zodiac (which it does not own) where that planet is "treated like a god", or exalted. It is always opposite its sign of debilitation. See Table 2 below.

Debilitation

Each planet has a sign in the zodiac (which it does not own) where that planet is "treated like a dog", or debilitated. It is always opposite its sign of exaltation. See Table 2 below.

Combustion

Combustion occurs when a planet is in such close proximity to the Sun that it becomes invisible, ie, eclipsed by the corona of the Sun. Orbs (zones) of effective combustion vary by planet. See Table 4 below.

Planetary war

Planetary war, or *graha yuddha*, occurs when two of the five natural planets are found within one degree of longitude of each other. By definition, the Sun and Moon are never involved in planetary war, nor are the Moon's nodes Rahu and Ketu.

Friend

The basic rule says, two planets are friendly when the signs they own are trine to each other. Eg, the Sun, Mars and Jupiter are friends because their fire signs Leo, Aries and Sagittarius are all in a trinal (1-5-9) relationship. Similarly for the Moon, Mars and Jupiter whose water signs are trinal. And again for Mercury, Venus and Saturn, no matter whether you consider their earth signs or air signs. For some variations, see Table 3 below.

Enemy

Certain planets (for reasons too complex to easily explain) are deemed inimical to each other's nature. See Table 3 below.

Retrograde

When planets in their orbits are closer to the Earth, they may temporarily appear to move backwards against the background of the fixed stars and the zodiac. Because of their relative proximity, they also appear brighter during their period of retrogression and are therefore considered to exert greater effects as per their nature.

Eclipse

Eclipses occur when the Sun, Moon and Earth are aligned. Solar eclipses occur when the Moon comes between the Earth and the Sun, temporarily blocking our view of the Sun. Lunar eclipses occur when the Earth comes between the Sun and the Moon, and its shadow covers the Moon.

Dig bala

Technically, not an *avastha* as per classic definition, but a planet enjoys directional strength when: Mercury and/or Jupiter is in the 1st house, the Moon and/or Venus in the 4th, Saturn in the 7th, the Sun and/or Mars in the 10th. Under the same principle, Mars' proxy Ketu gains *dig bala* in the 10th, while Saturn's surrogate Rahu gains *dig bala* in the 7th.

Table 2: Signs of ownership, exaltation & debilitation

Planet	Own sign	Mooltrikona	Exaltation	Debilitation
Sun	Leo	Leo	Aries	Libra
Moon	Cancer	Cancer	Taurus	Scorpio
Mars	Aries, Scorpio	Aries	Capricorn	Cancer
Mercury	Gemini, Virgo	Virgo	Virgo	Pisces
Jupiter	Sagittarius, Pisces	Sagittarius	Cancer	Capricorn
Venus	Taurus, Libra	Libra	Pisces	Virgo
Saturn	Capricorn, Aquarius	Aquarius	Libra	Aries
Rahu	... nil ...	... nil ...	Scorpio	Taurus
Ketu	... nil ...	... nil ...	Scorpio	Taurus

Table 3: Friends, enemies & neutrals

Planet	Friends	Neutrals	Enemies
Sun	Moon, Mars, Jupiter	Mercury	Venus, Saturn
Moon	Sun, Mercury	Mars, Jupiter, Venus, Saturn	... nil ...
Mars	Sun, Moon, Jupiter	Venus, Saturn	Mercury
Mercury	Venus, Saturn	Sun, Mars, Jupiter	Moon
Jupiter	Sun, Moon, Mars	Saturn	Mercury, Venus
Venus	Mercury, Saturn	Mars, Jupiter	Sun, Moon
Saturn	Mercury, Venus	Jupiter	Sun, Moon, Mars
Rahu	... nil ...	... nil ...	... nil ...
Ketu	... nil ...	... nil ...	... nil ...

Table 4: Effective orbs of combustion

Planet	When in direct motion	When retrograde
Mercury	14°	12°
Venus	10°	8°
Mars	17°	17°
Jupiter	11°	11°
Saturn	15°	15°

Appendix 2: Other major yogas based on lordship

This is *not* an exhaustive catalogue of yogas, rather a very limited set of definitions for those yogas frequently cited in Part 2, whose specifications occasionally vary from book to book.

Dharma Karma Adhipati Yoga

Dharma Karma Adhipati Yoga is formed when the lord of a *trikona* combines with the lord of a *kendra* via association or mutual aspect. Many astrologers, despite knowing this definition, also refer to this as a *raja yoga*.

Raja Yoga

When I use the term *Raja Yoga*, it's typically in the limited context of BPHS Chapter 41, Verse 33-34: when the 5th and 9th lords are joined by association or mutual aspect.

Occasionally, I will also use the same term, albeit in a more generic sense, to denote the yoga that is formed when (i) a *trikona* lord combines with one of the nodes in a *kendra*, or (ii) a *kendra* lord combines with a node in a *trikona*. In either case, the node acts as proxy for its dispositor which, if it were indeed present, would form a *Dharma Karma Adhipati Yoga* with the other planet.

Dhana Yoga

Dhana Yoga is formed when the lord of a *dhana*/money house (2, 11) combines by association or mutual aspect with the lord of a *trikona* house (1, 5, 9).

A more liberal definition allows any combination of lords of 1, 2, 5, 9 and 11. Thus, lords of 2nd and 11th could form *dhana* yoga. Likewise, lords of 5th and 9th could form it (although Parashara has already called this combo a *raja yoga*.)

I prefer the more restrictive definition. *Dharma Karma Adhipati Yoga* requires one planet from each of the *kendra/trikona* group. Similarly, *Dhana Yoga* should require one from each of the *trikona/dhana* groups.

In the context of this book, *Dhana Yoga* is only formed with *trikona* and *dhana* lords in *sambandha*, not just two *trikona* lords, nor two *dhana* lords.

Viparita Yoga

A common form of *Viparita Yoga* arises when the lords of two *trikasthanas* occupy other *trikasthanas* without necessarily exchanging houses.

Another variety of *Viparita Yoga* arises when *trik* lords combine by association or mutual aspect – regardless of what houses they occupy. For example, if the 6th lord and 8th lord are in mutual aspect from the 5th and 11th houses, that's also *Viparita Yoga*.

This form of *Viparita* Yoga is functionally "pure" only so long as the two *trik* lords don't contaminate the positive houses. This means that a third planet owning positive houses can't be in association or mutual aspect with either of those *trik* lords.

To preserve the *Viparita Yoga*'s classic "reversal of misfortune" theme, the two *trik* lords can only be in *sambandha* with each other, or in contact with a third *trik* lord or the Rahu-Ketu axis. Another *trik* simply keeps it in the family, while the nodes without lordship can't spread collateral damage to positive houses.

Appendix 3: The Statistics of *Parivartana Yoga*

Methodology

My original analysis for this thesis was made possible with the use of Lois Rodden's AstroDatabank 2.1 which on its release contained 23,107 records of personal and mundane data.

By filtering the database to retain only charts with Rodden Rating "AA" data (recorded by family or state) or "A" (quoted by the person, kin, friend or associate), this netted 7406 famous people, 2886 private citizens, and 4717 anonymous individuals, for a total of 15,009 more-or-less-accurate charts.

A second filtering process applied to these 15,009 charts identified 6403 *Parivartana Yogas* among them. On the surface, this implied roughly 43% of the general population has a *Parivartana Yoga*.

An identical filtering process applied only to the 7406 "famous" people identified 3170 *Parivartana Yogas* among them. As with the general population, this implied roughly 43% of the famous had a *Parivartana Yoga*.

When I examined the individual data more closely, however, I found that a certain percentage of people had more than one *Parivartana Yoga*. Of the 3170 famous people with the yoga, 243 of them had more than one.

By discarding double (and triple) counts, I found 2927 people with one or more *Parivartana Yogas*, roughly 40% of the "famous" population. Because individual data inspection is time-consuming, I didn't duplicate this analysis for the larger population, but assumed more or less equivalent results.

Therefore, as *jyotishis* we should expect to see many clients with a *Parivartana Yoga*, since almost four out of 10 charts will have at least one. On the other hand, a chart with two or more such yogas is relatively rare, since little more than 3% of the population fall in this category.

Taking this one step further, seeking charts with three *Parivartana Yogas*, I found only two people out of the 7406 famous subjects. In other words, this is rare, generally occurring only three times out of 10,000.

Observations

Although I subsequently went on to examine the frequency with which the 66 varieties of *Parivartana Yoga* occurred in this "famous" population, a chi-squared test of these frequencies did not reveal anything statistically significant. However, I did make the following observations:

- Of the ten *Parivartana Yogas* most frequently found in the charts of the famous, half of them (in their pre-exchange state) also form other major yogas, such as *Dharma Karma Adhipati, Dhana* and *Viparita Yogas*. Four out of ten also involve the *lagnesh*, arguably the most significant house lord of the chart. The fourth lord alone made no appearance in any of those ten yogas.

- Of the ten *Parivartana Yogas* least frequently found in the charts of the famous, only two formed other major yogas. Only two out of ten involved the *lagnesh*. The fourth lord, along with the sixth lord, was best represented in these ten yogas.

What can we hypothesize about the necessary prerequisites of fame, at least insofar as they might be indicated via *Parivartana Yogas*? The list is brief:

- *Parivartana Yoga* takes on greater power when the two house lords participate in other yogas.

- Participation of the ascendant lord (identity, ego, personality) is an important factor in generating fame.

- The lord of the 4th (education, ethics, happiness) is not an important factor in generating fame.

BIBLIOGRAPHY

Agarwal, G.S. *Practical Vedic Astrology*. New Delhi, India: Sagar Publications, 1998.

deFouw, Hart & Svoboda, Robert. *Light on Life*. London, England: Penguin Books, 1996.

Feuerstein, Georg. *The Shambhala Encyclopedia of Yoga*. Boston, USA: Shambhala Publications, 1997.

Kapoor, Deepak. *Prashna Shastra, Volume I*. New Delhi, India: Ranjan Publications, 1999.

Krishnamurti, K.S. *Horary Astrology: Advanced Stellar System*. Madras, India: Mahabala Publishers, 1970.

Levacy, William. *Beneath a Vedic Sky*. Carlsbad, USA: Hay House Inc, 1999.

Mantreswara. *Phala Deepika*. Translated S.S. Sareen. New Delhi, India: Sagar Publications, 1992.

Monier-Williams, Sir Monier. *A Sanskrit-English Dictionary*. New Delhi, India: Motilal Banarsidass Publishers, 2002.

Parashara. *Brihat Parashara Hora Shastra, Volume I*. Translated Girish Chind Sharma. New Delhi, India: Sagar Publications, 1995.

Raman, B.V. *Three Hundred Important Combinations*. Delhi, India: Motilal Banarsidass Publishers, 1997.

LIST OF CASE STUDIES

All data can be confirmed by accessing the Astrodatabank website at http://www.astro.com/astro-databank/Main_Page

Angelou, Maya. 04 April 1928, 14h10 CST, Saint Louis, Missouri.

Baker, Josephine. 03 June 1906, 11h00 CST, Saint Louis, Missouri.

Beatty, Warren. 30 March 1937, 17h30 EST, Richmond, Virginia.

Bell, Alexander Graham. 03 March 1847, 07h00 LMT, Edinburgh, Scotland.

Belli, Melvin. 29 July 1907, 08h00 PST, Sonora, California.

Bernhardt, Sarah. 23 October 1844, 20h00 LMT, Paris, France.

Bukowski, Charles. 16 August 1920, 10h00 CET, Andernach, Germany.

Carlin, George. 12 May 1937, 11h45 EDST, New York, New York.

Catherine, the Great. 02 May 1729, 02h30 LMT, Stettin, Germany.

Cézanne, Paul. 19 January 1839, 01h00 LMT, Aix, France.

Cleese, John. 27 October 1939, 03h15 GDT, Weston-super-Mare, England.

Clinton, Hillary Rodham. 26 October 1947, 08h02 CST, Chicago, Illinois.

Coward, Noel. 16 December 1899, 02h30 GMT, Teddington, England.

Dass, Ram. 06 April 1931, 10h40 EST, Boston, Massachusetts.

De Beauvoir, Simone. 09 January 1908, 04h30 LST, Paris, France.

Dion, Céline. 30 March 1968, 12h15 EST, Charlemagne, Quebec.

Dylan, Bob. 24 May 1941, 21h05 CST, Duluth, Minnesota.

Einstein, Albert. 14 March 1879, 11h30 LMT, Ulm, Germany.

Farouk, King. 11 February 1920, 22h30 EET, Cairo, Egypt.

Farrow, Mia. 09 February 1945, 11h27 PDST, Los Angeles, California.

Flynn, Errol. 20 June 1909, 02h25 AEST, Hobart, Australia.

Folger, Abigail. 11 August 1943, 17h27 PDST, San Francisco, California.

Gacy, John Wayne. 17 March 1942, 00h29 CDST, Chicago, Illinois.

Gandhi, Indira. 19 November 1917, 23h11 IST, Allahabad, UP, India.

Hugo, Victor. 26 February 1802, 22h30 LMT, Besancon, France.

Johnson, Virginia. 11 February 1925, 09h30 CST, Springfield, Missouri.

Kennedy, Ethel. 11 April 1928, 03h30 CST, Chicago, Illinois.

Kerouac, Jack. 12 March 1922, 17h00 EST, Lowell, Massachusetts.

King, Stephen. 21 September 1947, 01h30 EDST, Portland, Maine.

Knievel, Evel. 17 October 1938, 14h40 MST, Butte, Montana.

Kubler-Ross, Elisabeth. 08 July 1926, 22h45 MET, Zurich, Switzerland.

Leno, Jay. 28 April 1950, 02h03 EST, New Rochelle, New York.

London, Jack. 12 January 1876, 14h00 LMT, San Francisco, California.

Madonna. 16 August 1958, 07h05 EST, Bay City, Michigan.

Manet, Edouard. 23 January 1832, 19h00 LMT, Paris, France.

Meher, Sri Baba. 25 February 1894, 05h00 LST, Poona, India.

Merton, Thomas. 31 January 1915, 09h00 GMT, Prades, France.

Minnelli, Liza. 12 March 1946, 07h58 PST, Los Angeles, California.

Montessori, Maria. 31 August 1870, 02h40 LST, Chiaravalle, Italy.

Navratilova, Martina. 18 October 1956, 16h40 MET, Prague, Czechoslovakia.

Nietzsche, Friedrich. 15 October 1844, 10h00 LMT, Rocken, Germany.

Nixon, Richard. 09 January 1913, 21h35 PST, Yorba Linda, California.

Page, Jimmy. 09 January 1944, 04h00 GDT, Heston, England.

Picasso, Pablo. 25 October 1881, 23h15 LMT, Malaga, Spain.

Plath, Sylvia. 27 October 1932, 14h10 EST, Boston, Massachusetts.

Rajneesh, Sri Bhagwan. 11 December 1931, 17h13 IST, Bhopal, MP, India.

Richards, Keith. 18 December 1943, 06h00 GDT, Dartford, England.

Rimbaud, Arthur. 20 October 1854, 06h00 LMT, Charleville, France.

Rodman, Dennis. 13 May 1961, 00h10 EDST, Trenton, New Jersey.

Rommel, Erwin. 15 November 1891, 12h00 LST, Heidenheim,

Germany.

Rudhyar, Dane. 23 March 1895, 01h00 LST, Paris, France.

Russell, Bertrand. 18 May 1872, 17h45 GMT, Trellech, Wales.

Schubert, Franz. 31 January 1797, 13h30 LMT, Vienna, Austria.

Silkwood, Karen. 19 February 1946, 21h50 CST, Longview, Texas.

Snowden, Edward. 21 June 1983, 04h42 EDST, Elizabeth City, North Carolina.

Spillane, Mickey. 09 March 1918, 00h10 EST, Brooklyn, New York.

Susann, Jacqueline. 20 August 1918, 19h25 EDST, Philadelphia, Pennsylvania.

Swift, Taylor. 13 December 1989, 20h46 EST, Wyomissing, Pennsylvania.

Trump, Ivana. 20 February 1949, 00h55 MET, Gottwaldov, Czechoslovakia.

Turner, Lana. 08 February 1921, 12h30 PST, Wallace, Idaho.

Turner, Ted. 19 November 1938, 08h50 EST, Cincinnati, Ohio.

Turner, Tina. 26 November 1939, 22h10 CST, Nutbush, Tennessee.

Waits, Tom. 07 December 1949, 07h25 PST, Pomona, California.

Westheimer, Dr. Ruth. 04 Jun 1928, 04h00 MET, Karlstadt, Germany.

Windsor, Queen Elizabeth. 21 April 1926, 02h40 GDT, London, England.

Winfrey, Oprah. 29 January 1954, 04h30 CST, Kosciusko, Mississippi.

ABOUT THE AUTHOR

Alan Annand is a Canadian astrologer, accredited by the American College of Vedic Astrology and the British Faculty of Astrological Studies. He consults, teaches and writes a monthly blog on a range of topics.

His book *Stellar Astrology* is a compilation of essays on techniques, in-depth celebrity profiles, and analysis of mundane events. This is an informative and entertaining reference work for serious students of astrology.

His *NEW AGE NOIR* crime series (*Scorpio Rising*, *Felonious Monk*, *Soma County*) features astrologer and palmist Axel Crowe, whom one reviewer dubbed "Sherlock Holmes with a horoscope."

Websites: navamsa.com, sextile.com

CPSIA information can be obtained
at www.ICGtesting.com
Printed in the USA
BVOW06s0553211217
503315BV00022BA/2742/P